MEMOIRS OF A
RELUCTANT COPPER

Memoirs of a Reluctant Copper

Douglas Hemingway

To order additional copies of this book, contact:
Xlibris
800-056-3182
www.Xlibrispublishing.co.uk
Orders@Xlibrispublishing.co.uk
759628

Contents

PROLOGUE

———————

I suppose I should say from the beginning that the views expressed hereinafter are not necessarily the views of the Metropolitan Police or any of its members, employees, and office holders. Indeed, many of them would disagree with me, but they'd be wrong.

I will not use official statistics because, statistically, 100 per cent of all published statistics are meaningless. They are meaningless because those who use them will twist them to make them say whatever shows that individual in a good light. I will use my experiences, but I will not say anything that would identify who, where, or when a particular incident happened. This is to protect the innocent and observe the Data Protection Act. The examples I use are, however, accurate and are taken from personal experience.

I will not hold back on who I think are barking up the wrong tree and why. I will always try to justify my comments, something that some of the people with whom I deal do not feel necessary. Why reluctant? Is it because I was reluctant to do the job in the first place? No. Is it because I am reluctant to do the job now that I am established? Definitely not.

In the following pages, I will try to explain this title. I was never the natural policeman. I am a bit dizzy on occasions. I am not a 'rules-is-rules' kind of a guy. I am comfortable with what I do for a living, but I do not necessarily want to talk about it when I am away from work.

In a job that can be as intense as this, and a job that invokes so much passionate discussion, one needs to take time out as often as possible.

All my friends are drawn from other lifestyles, professions, and belief structures for this very reason. I do not shirk my responsibilities when I am off-duty. If I see something happening, I will deal with it appropriately without putting myself in danger, but I don't actively look for trouble. My friends tell me that I am not the typical police officer. Those who I do not tell about my profession remain blissfully ignorant because I do not come across as an officious knob, and that is what people expect when they do not know police officers outside of their working environment. Indeed, I know a few that are officious knobs and try to throw their weight around in private life while out in pubs, while on the rugby field, and are people who I avoid. So these pages are an attempt to try to figure out why I became a police officer, why I seem to enjoy what I do despite myself, and why I appear to be reasonably decent at what I do.

Can I also say that most criminals are stupid? If they weren't stupid, they would be rocket scientists, but they are not. This is all very fortunate because in my experience, a lot of coppers are pretty dim too (present company included). If criminals were clever, we would all be in deep trouble.

I have subtitled many paragraphs. These are little stories that I hope will demonstrate the different struggles that I went through. Some are humorous, some angry, and some just factual. All, I hope, are entertaining and I hope will give an insight into my working life and how I think.

I should also say that I started writing this in 2012. Laws change, as do procedures. Even belief systems adjust. The Met Police is in a constant state of flux. This is mainly because senior ranking officers want to change things for the purposes of showing their masters that they can do stuff not because they want to improve matters. If things do improve, that would always be welcome—a surprise, but no less welcome.

A Potted History

I was born in Scotland and raised in transit. That is to say on the move, not in a Ford Transit van. Anyone who is now thinking 'raised in a Transit (van)', (chortle, chortle)... can stop right there. You aren't the first. It was funny the first 150 times. My father was a Yorkshireman born and bred probably not a million miles from where my family name originates. My mother was born in Romford, Essex (I never once saw her wearing white stilettos) and raised in and around the south-east of England. She was from seafaring stock, so I can probably trace that side of the family to all corners of the earth.

My parents met and married in the RAF. Mother left the RAF to raise the family. There were four kids: two girls and two boys. I was the second in line. My elder sister was born in Germany; my younger brother and I were born in St Andrews, Scotland; and the younger sister in Scampton, Lincolnshire. My dad left the RAF after sixteen years as a corporal. I believe he was always knocked back for promotion, as he was too opinionated and upset too many officers by contradicting them. It wasn't the fact of the contradiction that upset them, it was the fact that he, more often than not, turned out to be right. We can't be having rankers being more knowledgeable than the officers now, can we? Rank will always trump knowledge.

My father wanted to leave the country when he left the RAF. He would have gone to Norway if he had his own way. Too cold for Mother though, and she wouldn't have it. He had job offers in Cypress and

South Africa. He got the job in South Africa and off we went. I had started my schooling in Germany and continued in Norfolk, so SA was my third country as far as schooling was concerned.

It won't surprise people to know that South Africa in 1968 was intolerable. Everyone was racist. That is *everyone*, not just whites, not just Afrikaners—everyone. Blacks hated whites and insulted them at every turn, whites hated blacks, and Asians hated everyone. Afrikaners hated white people from any other background, oh and the blacks and Asians as well. Heaven only knows how the country operated on a day-to-day basis; it was like the worst dysfunctional family in the world. We left after thirty months and went to Zimbabwe.

There was a much better attitude towards each other there. Okay, everyone was racist. Everyone seemed to want to insult people, and no one wanted to mix socially outside their racial group, but they did seem to work well. No one was prevented from going wherever they wanted or going about their legal business unlike the South Africa of the late sixties and the seventies.

I will not say all was rosy. Most black people were prevented from advancing in the mainstream industries. If they were going to be successful, they had to do it privately. Preventing large swathes of any community from advancing themselves professionally and academically is never a wise way of conducting business because you miss out on talent. They didn't have the vote either, but then they don't have that even now. It was very much better than SA in any event, and it was our reality for that time. We eventually settled in Zimbabwe where I completed my schooling and went off to work on gold mines. I started off learning about surveying; that is, land surveying not head counting or quantity surveying. Essentially, I was trying to get tunnellers to tunnel in the right direction.

I gave that up to go into the engineering side. I did an apprenticeship then in 1983 and left Zimbabwe with the woman who was to become—and remain—my wife. The writing was on the wall as far as the country was concerned, and I could see that Zimbabwe was being run by a bunch of self-centred bigoted greedy politicians. Not entirely unlike the previous lot, although they were never greedy and they were sort of elected. I could see that it was all going to go wrong, so I left and came to England with my girlfriend. We eventually married, had kids, and we are still together. The rest of my family followed in dribs and drabs except my elder sister who lives in South Africa and my father who died out there.

We came to England with £176 between the two of us. That was all Zimbabwe allowed us to take. England in 1983 was in the grip of hard times. Unemployment was well over three million. Despite this, we both found work relatively easily doing whatever we had to do in order to survive: packing boxes, delivering furniture, digging out flooded basements, and so on. In the early days, we would go to the pub on a Friday night and share a half pint of lager to celebrate getting through another week. In all that time, we never really argued—there was no time for that—we just got on. This has carried through our lives. Although there is the odd squabble, they are always short-lived and few and far between.

I eventually became a copper and have made it my career. I have also developed skills in drawing and guitar playing among other things. These are just hobbies and are not done to any kind of high standard. My job is done to the highest standard that I can attain, and I do it to the best of my abilities.

When I am not working, I distance myself from the job I do. This is not through embarrassment or dislike of the job I do; it is because you cannot take a job like mine home. Too many coppers fall into the trap of thinking that everyone is the same as the people with whom we deal. Let's face it. We don't deal with nice people. One has to step away and realise that normal people are not scumbags, out to thieve or diddle you out of your life savings. I also find that many people have opinions about the work I do. Some of it is complimentary, some not. I find, when I am out trying to enjoy myself and relax, it doesn't do to start trying to defend my position or explain the finer points of this person's parking ticket or that person's brother who got himself into a spot of bother. It is easier to just not mention it unless specifically asked.

Many people with whom I associate probably don't even know what I do for a living because it just doesn't come up in conversation. I enjoy playing guitar, drawing caricatures of my colleagues and friends, fell-walking with my wife, keeping my brain active by doing cryptic crosswords, and solving logic problems. I do most of the cooking in the house, and I also like going to the pub and sampling the concoctions produced by local real ale breweries. None of this is related to what I do for a living. It allows me to step away from the grim reality of life and enjoy myself.

When I retire, I will probably leave London. I know too much about its underbelly, and I don't want to be anywhere near it when I don't have to be. As it is, I take every opportunity to get out of London during weekends. I know that every town, city, and rural community have their own 'underbelly', but I don't know about them, so I can blank it all out and look at these places from my own perspective. Almost like burying one's head in the sand, but at least I do it knowingly.

GETTING STARTED

M y early years are a bit of a blur with all those countries in such a short time. I suppose RAF and army brats know better than most what it is like growing up without the company of a pal that you have grown up with, done your schooling, met your first girl friend with, etc. At the age of 10, I arrived in Rhodesia (as was) having never known anyone to call a friend for more than a couple of years. I don't know if this was a good thing or a bad thing, but it definitely shaped my life subsequent to that.

Settling down in a sunny, underpopulated country was fantastic for a kid. All those open spaces, plenty of harmless mischief to get up to, and not much in the way of TV. There was one channel, and that was only on between 5.30 p.m. and 10.30 p.m. and didn't inspire in any case. We went everywhere by bicycle. Salisbury was the capital. It is now Harare, but that is where we lived. We grew up on what was considered the wrong side of the track. My father worked on aeroplanes, so we lived in an area that afforded easy access to the airport. Many of the people who lived in my area did the same thing.

I enjoyed playing rugby and cricket at school. I was better at rugby, so the deputy head always referred to me as Hemingway in the summer and Douglas in the winter to reflect my lack of cricketing prowess. I always had a never-say-die attitude when I was playing sport. The school rugby and cricket teams were not the best, so we were often defeated, but I could never understand why everyone had virtually given up by half-time. It was for this reason that I was always picked for teams. I always got stuck in. I was having huge fun.

I was never an angry child. I put this down to being able to relieve frustrations on the rugby field. On reflection, this was probably an excellent grounding for being a police officer. We are in a no-win business—make no mistake. We may win many battles, but the war will probably never be won. When I was working on fraud investigations, someone said to me that a half-decent fraudster would get away with £1000s each time he operates. The better he is, the more he will make. As an investigator, it doesn't matter how good I am, I won't make any more or lose anything. So who has the biggest motivation to succeed? I always did what I could, but if I didn't succeed, I just shrugged my shoulders and moved to the next job. This may seem a bit harsh, and the great and the good in senior positions in the police will doubtlessly draw a sharp intake of breath on hearing that, but that is life. They would probably never understand because they don't actually do the job anyway.

The group of boys that I hung around with at school could not be called a gang. We didn't have a name, and we never caused problems with other groups. We just hung out and did our own thing. I believe we had a bit of a reputation. I don't really know where it all came from, but we did not discourage it because it meant that other troublemakers left us alone. Living on the wrong side of the tracks meant that the school I went to was a bit frayed at the seams. Boys from other schools would be wary when meeting us, not because we were hard-arsed bastards, but because they *thought* we were hard-arsed bastards. There was never any such trepidation on the rugby field.

There follows a few examples of my youth in Zimbabwe. I think it is relevant as it gives an insight to my mindset at a very early age, although becoming a police officer couldn't have been further from my mind in Zimbabwe. It wasn't considered a good job and people only joined as an alternative to military service, but the seeds were being sewn.

DEPUTY HEAD'S ALLEGATION

I suppose it was at this time that I started getting my attitude towards right and wrong that eventually manifested itself in becoming a police officer. I recall having a discussion with my deputy headmaster one day towards the end of my school career. He was your archetypal Victorian English schoolmaster. He was tall, moustachioed, and had a very posh colonial booming voice. Spare the rod;, spoil the child. He didn't spoil the child...ever!

He spoke to me about drug use once. I was in his office. I can't remember why I was in his office. I was there so often for some indiscretion or another. On this occasion, the fact that he was accusing me of using drugs was thinly veiled. He never actually said it out loud, so I could never deny it—not that it would make any difference. He was the deputy head, he was always right, and I was *always* wrong. As it happened, I never used any illegal substances. I was smoking cigarettes at that time, but who wasn't? It was the 1970s! I was probably getting my hands on alcohol as well (who wasn't?), but never drugs.

I have tried to explain my attitude towards this subject with friends and colleagues. I am not sure that I have been entirely successful. It is not a concept that police officers easily grasp. I believe the *reason* for me not using drugs was wrong, but the *result* was right. I did not use drugs because it was illegal. 'Oh', I hear you say, 'what is wrong with that attitude?' Police officers will always say that this is a good attitude to have. I believe that it is not really sustainable. One should decide not to do things because they feel it is not right or proper, not just because it is illegal.

There are many stupid laws around that we all ignore as being stupid. None of us (or at least not many) say, 'Oh, but it's illegal, we shouldn't do it.' Even some laws that are there for good reason are routinely ignored by otherwise law-abiding people. Take speeding for example. Not many drivers out there can boast that they have never exceeded the speed limit. The majority only keep the limit for fear of getting caught not because it is illegal. If one thought about it, most of the traffic laws are routinely ignored by many otherwise law-abiding people. I think it is because basic laws like theft, assault, or damaging of property are ingrained into our unconscious minds. We don't have to think about it, we just know.

Traffic laws are very recent and a little abstract. Although when one thinks about it, they are there to protect other road users, but what is one doing when they go through a red traffic light at 3 a.m. when there is no one around? I am not advocating jumping red lights, but you get my drift. If you walked past a motorcar with the engine running and no one in sight, consider what your very first thought is. Not your considered thought or anything like that nor what you think you might actually do, just the very first thought that pops into your head. Most people will think, 'Where is the stupid prat? He will have that car stolen if he isn't back soon.' Some may even think, 'I'll nick that car just to teach him a lesson.' But they never actually do it. Then there are the one who will think, 'I could nick that car, and the owner would never catch me.' This is the difference between a criminal mind and an honest one. It would never enter the mind of an honest person to steal the car, although he would know that someone else would. That honest person does not steal that car or even think about it because he just does not think that stealing is the right way to live, not because it is against the law. This is why I think the *reason* for me not using drugs was probably the wrong one. The correct reason would be that it is just not good for me. The legality should be secondary and something that comes as a consequence of having the right attitude.

My headmaster was not the last person to accuse me of drug abuse. Some people in Zimbabwe thought that I must be a drug user because I was English, some just wanted to spread mischievous rumours. None of them affected my own thoughts and beliefs. There was a lot of drug use going on around me, but I just politely declined and carried on. Of course, I never considered all this at the time, but reflecting on it all and working through what I was thinking, what I was doing, and what others were doing around me makes me believe that the seeds were being planted very early in my life. Had I taken up the baton there and then, I would have made the worst copper in the world. I would have been officious and unbending. Fortunately, I didn't even come close to thinking about it then. I'd had a little life experience under my belt when I did start thinking about it, and this has stood me in good stead.

OLD BINGE DRINKER ME

I had a couple of brushes with the law during my life in Zimbabwe. The first was when I went to the stock car races in Glammis Stadium in Harare. There was a whole group of us. It was a lovely sunny day, and we all settled down to an afternoon of beer drinking and watching people trash their cars. I was first up for buying the beers so off I went. I got the round in and passed them around. I then sat down and took a sip of my beer. I was sitting a little away from my group. I can't remember why. I was immediately approached by plain-clothed police officer who asked how old I was. To this day, I don't know what it was all about. I find it hard to believe that the top brass would have sanctioned an operation and use up the valuable time of police officers just to arrest otherwise law-abiding youngsters, who were causing no problems and probably doing exactly what they were doing five years previously. I don't recall my response, but the fact was that I was six months away from my eighteenth birthday. I was arrested and spent the evening in what could only be described as a drunk tank at the local police station.

There were about twelve others who had suffered the same fate, although none from my group. I was, by no means, the youngest person being criminalised. One of the other guys who were arrested was two days off his eighteenth birthday! None of us had drunk anymore than a couple of mouthfuls, so we were not drunk. We were all taken to the police station and put into one large cell to contemplate our navels, while they decided on our fate.

We all had to wait for parents to arrive before they would release us. My father was a member of a bridge club, and he was not going to have his bridge game interrupted by a snotty-nosed little drunk, so I had to wait hours before he finally rolled up. I think I was the last one standing. I don't think he was overly upset, I just think he wanted to teach me a lesson. We all got away with a warning and went back to the pub to have a drink and discuss the relative merits of being a drunkard. Lesson definitely not learned there!

THE GREAT FIRE OF HARARE

The second time was somewhat more serious for all sorts of reasons. I will set the scene. My friends, my brother, and I were all at a disco local to our area. One of my friends had just been hoiked out of the police force on what they referred to as a dishonourable discharge—nothing illegal or corrupt or anything like that. I think he just got up to too much mischief, and the senior police officers grew tired of his antics. There were a couple of on-duty, uniformed police officers at the disco, making sure that we were all being sensible law-abiding citizens. While most of us were attempting to polish our metaphorical haloes, my friend couldn't help himself and kept on having a go at them. There was nothing malicious or insulting, just snide little digs every now and again. When it was time to leave the disco, the two officers set-up a roadblock at the exit to the disco. It was a cricket ground, and the driveway was quite long. Of course, being a cricket ground, it was flat and treeless, so we could see what was happening at the exit.

They had decided to stop each and every car exiting the premises. There was a long queue of cars waiting to get out. We knew instinctively that they were after us. I was the driver, and I certainly had too much to drink and was not properly licensed anyway. We took the sensible decision to leave the car and walk. Nothing much they could do about a small group of youngsters walking home after a few quiet drinks at the local disco. It was October time. This time of year in that part of Africa is very, very dry. The winter is always completely dry, and October is when everyone is anticipating the first rain. It is always hot and everything is tinder dry, bush fires are commonplace,. The smallest spark from a cigarette is all you need. A heated exchange of words in the vicinity of this sort of grass and hedge could start a fire.

Next to the cricket ground is a car park to the municipal swimming pool. The swimming pool comes after that. It is outdoor, as are the majority of swimming pools in Zimbabwe, and it was surrounded by a tall, evergreen hedge. The distance from where all the cars were being stopped to this hedge was probably 150 yards or more (i.e., the length of a cricket field and a substantial car park). We had probably walked about half the length of the cricket field when we noticed that one of our numbers was missing. We turned and saw my brother standing at the roadblock watching what the police were doing. He wasn't doing anything. He was just being a slightly annoying needle in their side.

We turned and went to get him. We didn't want to wind them up any more than we already had. We got back to where the officers were, and I struck up a conversation with a plain-clothed officer who just happened to be there. We were there for about five minutes when we turned to see the hedge around the swimming pool go up in flames. Due to the dryness of everything, this would have gone up in seconds. Possibly started by some bloke flicking his fag, or a lit match out the window of his car. That did not enter the minds of the uniformed officers whose names were—and I am not making this up—Gardener and Flowers! All they saw was an opportunity to get their own back.

We were all promptly arrested for arson and taken to the police station. We were all interrogated Sweeney-style by the scruff of the necks up against the wall in separate rooms. 'Why were you hanging around?' 'Who started the fire?' 'Your mate told us that you did it!' There was no doubt that they knew we could not have started the fire, and I, even as an 18-year-old boy, knew it. I don't believe I was intimidated because I knew of my own innocence. My only real concern was that they could somehow convince others by planting evidence. One of my friends had apparently said that they were simply waiting for his father to come and pick us all up. This was a rather large and somewhat risky porky.

Flowers decided to call his bluff and called his father. Fortunately, his father was thinking on his feet and confirmed the story. He then came to pick us up. Being the deputy chief fire officer for Zimbabwe, he was not used to police officers treating him with disrespect. When he arrived and got shitty attitude in spade loads from the officers, he gave them the severest dressing down that I have witnessed. I don't know what happened, but it definitely went up the chain of command. We obviously walked away without a stain on our characters. I never did find out how the fire was started.

I was recently talking to one of that number, the son of the fire chief. I didn't realise that his father was sent a number of subliminal messages from the police service after that—a little reminder or two not to interfere in the future. I am told he was told to come to a police station to stand in an identity parade where the police were looking for a robber. He was never picked out despite the fact that he was a forty something white male, and all the other people in the line-up were young, black males. He was never in danger of being charged. It was just a little message to say, 'Look what we can do if we wanted!'

Such was Zimbabwe. I left school and landed a job within weeks. I left home to work in the gold mines. I got to live in the tiniest communities in remote locations and basically learned how to become a human being. Those remote communities were fine. They all went to work either on the mines or in their farms during the day and went to the sports club during the evening and got drunk. There were probably a lot of extramarital affairs going on, but I was too young and inexperienced to understand all that. I was 17, and I hadn't a clue.

When I travelled back to Harare and met my friends, I increasingly found everyone just wanted to get drunk or stoned, often at the same time. I could do the drinking, but the getting stoned didn't interest me. It was a turbulent time in Zimbabwe. The Ian Smith regime was in its final year.

Rural Zimbabwe was a dangerous place. The war was never fought in the towns. Local remote villages were descended upon and pillaged by the freedom fighters, as they liked to call themselves. They were raped and pillaged and left in fear only to be descended upon by the government forces that would be interrogating them for info on the insurgents (Geneva convention was never really observed if you get my drift), so the poor villagers who just wanted to live in peace got it from all sides. Civilian cars were attacked on the rural roads, and even two civilian aircraft were shot down and the survivors murdered. I lost a friend who was a 15-year-old girl when she was being driven with her family to a holiday resort in the north.

I met Shirley sometime in 1980. We started dating properly in 1982 after we'd known each other for about a year. We then started hanging around in a group for another year before we took the plunge. I left the mining industry and returned to the big city. I stuck around for about six months and decided that I would come to the motherland with Shirley for a year. I'm still here.

ENGLAND

The year is 1983. Shirley - who will eventually become my wife and mother to my two sons - and I are bronzed and fresh from Zimbabwe. Shirley was born in Zambia (then Northern Rhodesia), but moved to Zimbabwe (then Southern Rhodesia) when she was a baby. She had never been to north of the Zambezi River since. We arrived in England in August. The weather had been warm until a few days earlier but was—to our unacclimatised bodies—cold.

We knew no one. Any relatives that I had in the country were effectively forgotten. There was no way I was going to land on their doorstep unannounced. We were to meet a person who was an acquaintance of Shirley's mother, and we were to stay there initially. We had no job prospects, we had our £176 in our pocket, and we had no clue as to how we were going to survive. Thinking about it now, we must have been certifiable! I would never do it now or advise anyone to do it now—except for my sons, of course, anything to get them out the house and on their own two feet.

We stayed at the woman's house for a week. She was starting to become very unwelcoming very early on and was starting to insist that Shirley find a live-in nanny job. This was not going to happen. The only thing that we had was us. We were not going to split up. We moved from there to a very kind man's house. He was an acquaintance of Shirley's sister and was happy to have us stay there for a short period.

He helped us to get work and found us a bedsit. We were off and running.

It was tough at first. We were earning £50 a week and spending £35 of that on rent. The rest went on food and electricity. We packed boxes, delivered furniture, and did manual labour. We didn't care what the work was as long as it was honest and paid our rent. We made a promise to ourselves in those early days that whatever happened we would always eat properly. Beyond that, we had no plans. We walked into our first bedsit with two backpacks. These held the sum total of our worldly possessions.

THRILLER IN SHEPHERD'S BUSH

Our first telly came as a direct result of Michael Jackson. My sister decided that England was the place for her. She landed and came to stay with us for a very short period of time. She couldn't believe how we got from one week to the next, but Michael Jackson's 'Thriller' was just coming out and was going to be shown on TV the very next day, not seeing it was not an option for my sister. Problem! We could barely afford to breathe, we didn't have a stereo, and a TV was just pie in the sky. We had not even considered it. We had come from Zimbabwe where TV was not at the forefront of everyone's lives, so we had never found it a problem being without. We couldn't afford to go to a pub to see it either. Not all that many had TVs anyway. We had to go and get one. £15 in our hands, and we were off to buy a TV. A black and white one, of course, but a TV nevertheless. 'Thriller' was then watched, and the world did not stop turning on its axis. Disaster averted.

THE TEA LEAF

On one occasion, on one of our weekly visits to the pub to share a half pint, we met an interesting character who entertained us with tales of his life. He was a bit of a prestidigitator and showed us some of his tricks. We didn't realise that while he was doing this, he was also picking our pockets for our door key. The next day, we went to work, and this man sent his buddies to go and break into our bedsit. This was a man who knew our circumstances, but still felt the need to steal the £160 of our rent money, leaving us with nothing for a week. It was then I realised that thieves were not *Robin Hood* characters, who were otherwise decent people who had fallen on hard times and only stole from people who could afford to lose a few possessions. Your average thief will steal anything from anyone because they are too lazy to go and get it for themselves legitimately.

Most of them talk about socialism but are, in fact, the ultimate capitalists. Everything is 'gimme, gimme, gimme'. They are not charitable, they do not share, and they do not care about anyone but themselves. They bang on about people being able to get it all back on insurance, and this seems to make it okay. Well, it isn't. How many people go to the insurers when some arse wipe has broken into their house and stolen £200 worth of stuff? No one. How many of those people feel unsafe in their houses regardless of how much has been taken? All of them!

The burglary was never solved, but my views on thieves, which were never all that charitable in the first place, became one of utter abhorrence. When we moved out a couple of years later, we needed a couple of suitcases. Our possessions were starting to grow, and we were getting ourselves established. We moved into another bedsit, which was just an owner-occupied house where the owners lived upstairs and we lived in the lounge. They were a delightful elderly Jamaican couple called Mr and Mrs Waite ('still waiting', he would often tell me). We stayed there for another few years.

We were now able to go to a pub and have a few beers without worrying about where our next meal was coming from. Our local was the Askew Arms. On reflection, it was a rough, old pub. A den of thieves and drug pushers, if ever there was one. I remember once being in there with my wife playing darts with the locals when a female came in and launched an attack on Shirley out of the blue. Shirley is the mildest-mannered person one would ever hope to meet, and this was clearly a case of mistaken identity.

To a man, every person came to the assistance of Shirley before any damage was done. There was no breast-beating, no desire to be a hero, they were just looking after a person who was one of their community and no outsider would interfere with that. I never witnessed drugs being bought and sold there, but I do remember walking in there one Saturday afternoon to find one of the regulars snorting cocaine directly off the bar surface. I valued my health, so I didn't say anything of it, but I didn't go in there as often after that.

THE EPIPHANY

I was walking in the road one day in Notting Hill Gate when I saw two uniformed police officers walking the beat. They weren't doing anything special, just walking the beat, chatting to passers-by. I thought to myself that I could do that. How difficult could it be to walk around telling people the way to the tube station? I had virtually no contact with police in England. I had those brushes with the law in Zimbabwe, but nothing in England. I recalled how we were dealt with when our home was burgled. It was courteous and professional without being overly officious. I felt that this was a way out of the situation that I was in. It was not a particularly bad situation, it was just not going anywhere.

I decided there and then to go for it and apply to join. At that point in time, I had not considered my upbringing or questioned why. It came down to nothing more than the thought of a safe and secure job that you didn't need any particular skill to do. I wasn't interested in driving cars fast with blue lights and sirens blaring. The idea of investigating crime didn't occur to me. I didn't think about tackling violent people. I am not a violent person. To this day, I can only remember hitting four people, and one of them was my brother, so that doesn't count.

There is a question that is always asked by potential employees, and that is, 'Why do you want to do this job?' It is a very important question, especially for the police. There are plenty of people out there who are power-hungry and see a uniform as being their conduit. It is a question that is seldom answered honestly either. 'I want to help the community' or 'I want to help people to feel safe' is a couple of responses one often hears. No one says, 'I want to drive police cars' or 'I heard some women go for men in uniforms'. I certainly did not respond in that manner. Even if that was what I wanted, I would not have responded in that manner. The fact is I couldn't really answer it satisfactorily and honestly, so I winged it. I can't remember how I answered it, but they clearly accepted it as sufficient for their needs.

In any event, I applied to and joined the police service in 1987. There was a two-day selection process, which was residential. It involved a written test, a fitness test, and several other things like medicals, eye tests, etc. The men had to be 5' 8" plus, and I sneaked in at 5' 9". My left eye was a bit dodgy, so I had to wear their glasses. I never did, but they thought I did so that was fine. The interview was stressful, but the good thing was that they told you that day if you had been successful. I spent twelve years in uniform, then became a detective where I continue to upset senior officers by being right all the time. The acorn does not fall far from the oak tree.

HENDON

At the time of joining, I had been married for fifteen months. Shirley had a decent job at a typesetting company. We had to move out of our bedsit. The police at that time were particular about where you lived. The police service owned a lot of real estate and housed most officers. There were single quarters dotted around London for the bachelors and blocks of police flats where young families were housed. I was effectively required to move into a police block of flats. Before I could contemplate this, I had to go through twenty weeks of initial training at the police training college in Hendon. As I write this, the college is in its final death throes, but when I started, there was a whole lot going on. It was the centre of excellence for the training of recruits, detectives, and drivers. There were promotions courses and other developmental courses of every type.

It was also a disciplined place. It was a residential course, so I was there for twenty weeks and only left the base on Friday afternoons to go home to the wife. We all had to wear full uniforms with helmets whenever we were outside. We had to wear tunics until the signal from the bosses that it was 'shirt sleeve order', which meant that, until further notice, we could wear long-sleeved shirt and tie. We had to salute all officers of inspector and above when outside and wearing a hat.

During class time, whenever we needed to get to another part of the complex, we had to march in our class group. There were no exceptions. We had to be smart at all times, our shoes shined, and our clothes ironed. Our hair had to be regulation short, back and sides, for the men and either short or tied back for the women. We were also required to maintain a level of fitness, so there were gym sessions at least twice a week. We had to get a lifesaving certificate, so there were swimming sessions every week. I am not sure how they handled the non-swimmers, but I was not one, so I just continued and got all my certificates. All of this is perfectly reasonable.

The police is a disciplined service. This is what we are told. I have often heard officers scoff at the thought of this concept. I think they miss the point. It is not disciplined in the same way as the armed services. The army are trained to do as they are told and not to think about it. Decisions will be made by other people who are trained, and you just do as you are told. Lives depend on it including your own! Police officers have to think on their feet. Their discipline comes from a different place. It is self-discipline. It is their ability to act and do things without someone telling them what to do and when to do it every step of the way. The Hendon discipline taught you to work as an individual, as part of a small team, which was part of a larger team, then ultimately the largest team—the police service. But in Hendon, all was not as it seemed.

RACISM

I am now going to deal with one of my elephants in the room: racism. People may draw breath and think that I am sailing close to the wind. I don't think I am. The message has always got to be to treat *everyone* equally. George Orwell was being satirical when he wrote that some animals are more equal than others in his novel, *Animal Farm*. I will deal with this subject now because Hendon tried desperately to get it right. They have tried to for the entirety of my service. Despite their every effort, they didn't do that well at first and have been blundering around in the dark ever since.

I always felt that Hendon, in my recruit days, was not used to its best advantage. They did things like race diversity where we would get a talk by someone from a different cultural background. The fact of it was fine, but the reasons behind it were slightly less clear. I would have been fine with it if they were trying to teach us something that could be used practically in our new profession. Things like something I found out for myself some years later about oriental people. We were interviewing an oriental female, and she appeared to be smiling all the time. My colleague made mention of this, as it appeared to him that she wasn't taking it all very seriously. I was confused about the smiling because everything else she did showed that she was extremely concerned about her predicament. I found that some oriental people appear to be smiling when they are very nervous or in a high state of anxiety. It is more like gritting their teeth than smiling, but is easily misinterpreted. It is a kind of defence mechanism. 'Look at me, I am no threat to you' sort of thing.

I felt that Hendon were not trying to teach us anything at all. They were doing this just as a flag-waving exercise. 'Look at us, we not racist, we are teaching everyone how not to be racist!' They did not! Even if it was a serious attempt, which it wasn't, it would have been misplaced. No one is ever going to come out and say, 'Oh, by the way, I am deeply racist,' while they were in Hendon. It was the most politically correct place on the planet—nothing gender-specific, nothing that may be perceived as racially unacceptable, and nothing that would offend cultural minorities. If you were racist when you got there, you would be racist when you left. It didn't matter how many racial scenarios we went through. The trick was to identify the bad apples before they got into the police. If you did that effectively, then what is the need for racial diversity days?

This thing about offending other cultures is a point with which I often take issue. The very idea that a Muslim would be offended by someone celebrating Christmas is madness. Muslim people are, by definition, religious. Most religious people of any hue—at least those who aren't violent fundamentalists bend on making the world believe their own ignorance—find it odd that there are people out there who aren't religious. Far from being offended, they fully accept it even if they don't agree with the particular belief system being celebrated.

Ironically, Muslims and Jewish people are more ready to accept the existence of Jesus Christ than many who observe the Christmas festival. They think of him only as a profit, but they accept he existed. Many people who celebrate Christmas are not religious and do not accept that there was even was such a person as Jesus Christ. Indeed, there are people who would produce evidence that several different people of that period could lay claim to being that person. Anyone who comes into this country, and is offended by Christianity, has a problem on their hands. They are the ones who are bigoted. The majority of people who do kick up a fuss are white middle-class breast-beaters, who are embarrassed about our past and seem hell-bent on making all of us pay for the mistakes of our ancestors. Some have a political agenda. They will cherry-pick what they hear and try to make headlines on issues that just don't exist.

I am personally not religious in any way. It is my personal view that the vast majority of religions are divisive and create exclusivity. A concept that is based on faith alone has become something that people will take into an argument and use it to tell others that their belief structures are wrong. They base this on no evidence whatsoever. More people have died and are still dying as a direct result of religious intransigence than any other reason bar disease and old age. This includes all the major religions including Christianity and Islam. I do not support any of them, but I don't begrudge the followers their own viewpoint, and I don't believe that they should be allowed to judge anyone for their belief structure, secular or otherwise. Voltaire once said, 'I disagree strongly with what you say, but I will defend to the death your right to say it.' I agree with him.

THEIR BEST EFFORTS

Back in Hendon, each class was separated into groups of four, and we were expected to do our studying and homework together and complete projects together. This was all about getting people to work in teams. You had your team of four within the class, then you had your class in which you would work as a team against other classes.

There were eight classes in my intake, and all the classes were paired so that they would work as a team. Then you would have your entire intake that would work together against other intakes. It was not a very racially diverse place when I got there. Great efforts were being made to recruit and retain people from ethnic minorities. The problem was that they were just not applying to join.

I always applauded the efforts that were being made in this area, and I could see a slow momentum being gained in getting people to put pen to paper. What I did not really agree with was the idea that once they were in, they should be treated differently. Racism is about discriminating against someone on the basis of the colour of his /her skin. Many opportunities have been lost by overlooking people who would, or at least, could have been as good as or better than people who were chosen over them because of their ethnic origin. I fear that we are slipping into this situation all over again—only it is ethnic minorities that are being favoured.

I hear the people who tell me that we have to redress the balance, and this is the most acceptable way of doing it. The people who say this go on to ignore any argument against it. We need a level playing field. If we always go for the best person for the job, then the racial diversity will sort itself out.

Pro-discrimination is the way the politicians now deal with it all. They won't admit it because it flies in the face of anti-discrimination legislation, but it is still happening. It is an oxymoron of sorts. I am taking it that it means discrimination in favour of. If you discriminate in *favour* of one person on the basis of skin colour, it stands to reason that you discriminate *against* someone else on the same basis. Discrimination is a negative aspect. You cannot put a positive prefix in front of a negative and expect it to make a positive. It does not work like that. Only positives or double negatives (like 'anti' and 'racism') make positives. You wouldn't use the phrase pro-wife-beating and believe that this is a good thing. So in essence, someone who supports pro-discrimination is in favour of discrimination. If this is on a racial basis, that makes them a racist. Treat everyone equally and you won't have this issue. By all means, respect everyone's different cultures and belief systems and take them into account when dealing with them, but that should not prevent you from treating people even-handedly and on a level playing field.

There was one black guy in our class of twenty, who I will refer to as Officer C. I didn't think much of the man. He was a little lazy and didn't seem to like police. It never occurred to me at first, but I still had quite a strong Southern African accent, and the instructors were always testing me to see if they could bring out the racist in me because in their eyes, South African = racist, and it was just a matter of time before I inadvertently let the cat out of the bag. It never occurred to them that the metaphorical cat never existed.

So Officer C was put in my group. I didn't think anything of this at the time. He was just another bloke on the team. Then came the racial diversity scenarios. Who do you think might be the people they would get to act out each scenario? Me and Officer C of course. I recall one brief where I was to be racially abusive to demonstrate a piece of public order legislation. I followed my brief. I didn't go over the top, but I played the part. The instructors then commented afterwards that they felt my acting was a little too close to the mark. I then realised what was happening—they were testing me and trying to make me trip up. I never felt I had to be careful from there on, as I was always comfortable with my position on racism, and that I was not—as far as I was concerned—a racist. What then happened is that I became more and more comfortable in my position. I knew what was happening. Better the devil you know.

Another requirement that we had was to have a boxing match. It was felt that we had to know what it was like to be hit. Everyone was paired to people of their own weight and height. There was a height limit in those days, so I, at 5' 9", was one of the shortest people around. Officer C was tall, rangy, and athletic. He did 100 metres in eleven seconds and swam like a stone. Despite the obvious disparity in size, shape, and fitness, I was put with him for my boxing match. They made some mealie-mouthed excuse that there was no one else to pair me up with. This removed all doubt about what they were doing. I decided to go for him in the ring. He was taller, had a long reach, and was probably stronger than me. I didn't particularly want to be hit by him. In the end, I wasn't. I just went at him for two minutes. The round was brought to a halt, and I was told off for being too vigorous in the ring. I think they were just upset that I hadn't been hit.

Officer C didn't last long in the police. I believe he was required to resign within two years. I heard rumours, but nothing I ever bothered to substantiate. I was just glad he was out of the police—not because of the colour of his skin. There are many fine police officers of every colour and cultural background with whom I am proud to work. He was just lazy and unpleasant. Why did he want to be a police officer if he did like police in any case?

ETYMOLOGY AND IGNORANCE

The last word I will have on this for the time being has to do with language. Niger or Nigra (as in linear 'nigra'—the dark line that runs from the naval to the pubis in pregnant women) is Latin for black. The word 'nigger' is a derivation of that word. It is now considered deeply insulting by the majority and is just not used by most people. You regularly hear black people using the word quite widely, particularly American comedians. Some people don't like it, but few complain.

In my view, I would never complain unless someone is deliberately using the word—or any other word for that matter—to insult someone else. If the user is talking about his friends in those terms and feels that the friends involved are comfortable with his language, then who am I to tell him how to use his language or refer to his friends? We have to be aware of who is around us and make sure that what we say is not going to upset people unnecessarily. This is not just in terms of racism but also in any way. At the same time, the person who does get upset should get upset for the right reason; and if a person is clearly not being insulting, then there is no reason for anyone to get upset. I have three examples.

The first, I hope, is an urban myth. I heard that a white man went up to the service counter of his work canteen. He asked the black female canteen worker to do something for him that was not on the menu. He asked nicely and would have accepted no for an answer. As it happened, the staff member said it would be fine and went off to sort it out. He said, 'Thank you very much, you're a good egg.' I don't know the origins of that phrase, but someone who was not involved in the exchange complained, as they thought that the word 'egg' was cockney rhyming slang (egg and spoon means 'boon') and extremely insulting name for a black person. The fact was that the man was being complimentary and thanking the woman. It did not enter his mind that it could be considered racist. He was clearly not being racist, and the complaint should never have been given the dignity of being investigated. If it is not an urban myth, I hope it was resolved sensibly.

The next happened to two of my colleagues—both white. One of my contemporaries was a talented javelin thrower and, given the right training, could have been world class. He tells me that he beat Steve Backley in a school competition. Mr Backley went on to get professional coaching and was a world-beater. My colleague couldn't afford it and became a police officer. If he could have, who knows? Anyway, there he was at an athletics meeting that he was attending when another of my colleagues, a man who was the ultimate in political correctness, was walking nearby. He spotted the javelin man and called a friendly greeting over to him using the epithet 'Chucker'. Unfortunately, a black man was nearby at the time and thought that he had been insulted and the comment was aimed at him—as in spear chucker—which he considered racist. This third person did not challenge or take issue at the time. He wasn't interested that 'Chucker' responded to the greeting. He did, however, complain later on that the officer was being racist and an investigation was initiated. This poor, decent man was put through the wringer for that. He was clearly not being racist, and a simple enquiry by the complainant would have cleared it all up in seconds.

The last was a story that I feel really demonstrates how people just aren't thinking. This was, apparently, in Scandinavia. It was a board meeting for a private company. A man was addressing board members complaining about lack of resources and said that he could not operate with such a *niggardly* allowance. He was summarily suspended for the usage of outrageously racist language. The man was clearly not being racist in any way. He never once referred to race. The word 'niggardly' has its origins in the Germanic languages (*nicht*) and means 'nothing' or 'a very small amount'. It does not have anything to do with the Latin word for black. So a man's character was stained due to ignorance. All they had to do was to understand that the man was referring to the small budget, and he would never have gone through all that.

All this boils down to the fact that people will insult each other when they are upset. When one is insulting another, they would go for a characteristic that the 'insultee' is going to react to the most and is often the most obvious and something that they can do little about. Four eyes, for example, in a person who wears glasses; fatso for someone who is overweight; and so on. Some people, when there is nothing else to pick on, will go for the colour thing. I have been racially abused on many occasions by white people, black, Asian, Middle Eastern, the lot, and yes, members of minority races can be racist and often are. I personally have no problem with the colour of my skin, so the insult dies before it is born, and I am left thinking the person doing the insulting has already lost the argument because he is using an inconsequential characteristic of mine to detract from whatever issue he may have had. I can therefore ignore the insult and steer the person back to the point in question. Water off a duck's back. It would be nice if everyone could do the same. That way, racists would have nowhere to go.

THE NON-SMOKING GUN

While on this subject, I cover another related subject that I believe the lawmakers got wrong. It doesn't flow chronologically, but it follows on from the racial theme. There came a point where all those clever boffins decided—quite correctly, I believe—that some offences were made worse when there was a racial element to it. They decided in their finite wisdom to create an add-on to some offences like assaults (excluding GBH), harassment offences, public order offences, etc. Essentially, what they did was to say that if there was a racial element to these existing offences, then a two-year tariff should be added on to any sentence handed down. These did not include robbery, GBH, murder, rape, etc. because you can't add two years to life! What's the problem then? I will list them:

1. The biggie! It is relatively simple to prove simple assaults and such like. E.g., a chap is walking down the road whistling a happy tune, a smile on his face, and a nose that is straight and proud. Nasty man walks past and punches him in his nice, straight nose. Man is no longer whistling a happy tune, and his nose is plastered all over his face. Nasty man nearby is hurling insults and has claret all over his fist. Nasty man is arrested. Nasty man is charged. Nasty man goes to court. This is not rocket science! People will just plead guilty and throw themselves upon the mercy of the court. The way the new legislation has been put together means that if you were to tag on the extra element, you have to prove *all* the elements of the new offence that it creates. That is the main offence together with the racial element. If you fail in one element, you fail in all. So a court cannot, for example, say that you have proved an assault so we can convict on that. But you haven't convinced the court of the racial element, so we will convict on the lesser offence only. Or perhaps worse, the court is satisfied as to the racial element, but has not been convinced of the assault aspect. It has to be all or bust, so either a violent person who may or may not be racist, or a racist person who may or may not be violent can walk away without a stain on his character. Because of this, very few people are charged with the racially aggravated offence. Missed opportunity?

2. Where many people would plead guilty to the lesser offence, few would plead to the racially aggravated offence. This is because of the large increase in the tariff and the difficulty for the prosecution. Let us be clear. Even though an assault can fetch five years in prison theoretically, the reality is that almost no one is sent to prison for ABH unless the charge forms part of a larger issue. What you end up with is more expense in running the prosecution and higher acquittal rates. We also

have to consider the stigmatism attached to certain offences. If you have a conviction for a racially aggravated offence, your slate will never be wiped clean—another reason for not pleading guilty.

3. Yes, it is true that you can't add two years to a life sentence, but in this country, life does not mean life as far as time spent in custody. It normally means fifteen years, and you're out on licence for life. Even then, this is only for murder most foul. Rapes, robberies, and GBHs get much lower sentences. Life is almost unheard of in recent years for anything less than murder. I came across one rapist who had been given a life sentence to serve a minimum of six years. Although in fairness, he was still there fourteen years later because he was so dangerous and would reoffend. You can add two years onto fifteen or any of the lesser sentences. It is not so much the tariff that is the problem. It is the intelligence value. When the person is released and police have to deal with the person because they just can't help themselves reoffending, intelligence checks are carried out before we go to their address. It is always good to know what you are walking into.

It seems to me the legislation is like a shotgun with no cartridges. It all looks very impressive and very threatening, but there is little you can do to carry out the apparent threat. Why not have an either/or facility? The worst that will happen is a Newton hearing, which is where someone who has already pleaded guilty to an offence but disagrees with all the facts, and so seeks to mitigate the sentence. For example, if someone agrees that an assault was committed but disagrees that a weapon was used, The Newton Hearing is there to decide facts. The either/or facility is used in murder cases where a jury is given the option of convicting a lesser offence given all the circumstances, why not other offences?

I had no love for Hendon. For a start, I was split from my wife for the first time in five years. The people were all overly competitive in all the wrong areas. The work was okay, but I didn't feel I was achieving anything while I was there. No college is ever going to properly prepare you for the real world. They can tell you what to expect, but there is nothing like actually being there. Hendon would have been better employed just cramming us with legislation. By all means, please demonstrate your points using different scenarios, but just be minded that the legislation is one's basic tool. If one has the wording of a piece of legislation stuck in your head, it will always be there when you need it. When you are out on the street and something has happened, you know that there is something wrong, but you can't put your finger on it. All you have to do is go back to the basics and think of the wording of each offence. This will get you out of most situations.

Hendon, of course, felt that they were there to teach you how to be police officers. The instructors personified the phrase 'those who can't do, teach'. I personally learned everything parrot fashion. It is still there in the back of my brain somewhere and gets dredged up every now and again. I did not learn about my profession properly until I started becoming a competent detective. And I only started out in that direction after twelve years.

All that being said, I still think that we should have a Hendon of some sort. Recruits are basically sent straight out onto the street with 'tutor constables' or mentors or whatever they call themselves these days. These are mainly relatively inexperienced officers and will bring their lack of experience to the table. There is no consistency in the teaching, and it is all a matter of luck if a recruit is posted to a busy police station with competent tutors. The difference between being posted to Harrow and being posted to Croydon is huge.

Croydon is the most populous borough with all the problems of an inner city, but over a huge area. Officers are constantly running from one incident to the next. They deal with whatever they come across quickly and move on. They become good at thinking on their feet and resolving issues quickly. The leafy streets of Harrow are much quieter. Officers have more time to be thorough and become better at covering all the bases and thinking things through. A police college would at least have everyone starting off at the same level and being able to build on what they have learned.

HOUSING

———•———

On leaving Hendon, we had to leave our little bedsit and move to our new home. Fortunately, we were moved to a place on the Ridgeway in Wimbledon. This was a salubrious area that I would never have been able to afford at that time or anytime since, so we had no complaints. The flats were utilitarian, but they weren't bedsits. They were two and three-bedroom flats with a large communal lawn where growing families allowed their children to play with each other. We started our family there. It seemed to us the perfect place to raise a family. Plenty of other kids to play with, and all with like-minded families. There were issues and incidents there, but nothing that we felt uncomfortable about.

ONE HELLUVA BENCH PRESS

One incident was when I was trying to fix my rust bucket of a car. It was a Lancia Prisma—the sedan version of a Lancia Delta. The car was on jacks, and I was tinkering with something or other. The jacks were not as secure as I thought, and the entire car fell on my chest. I was unable to call out or do anything due to the overwhelming weight on my chest. One of the other residents happened to be sunning himself on the lawn nearby and saw what happened. He ran to the car and lifted it off my chest. I wriggled out relatively unharmed. The wheel arch of the car was rusted and jagged, and the car was a reasonable sized family

car. My saviour did not cut himself or hurt his hands in any way on the
lethal wheel arches nor could he lift the car afterwards. That same car
was broken into some time later. We never locked it. It wasn't worth
stealing. It also had a very noisy door. This door woke up another of my
fellow residents. He looked out his window, saw what was happening,
and ran down to confront him. He was knocked down and a chase
ensued—a chase in which the thief lost.

THE BIG WIND

We were there during the big storm that hit England in 1987 (I
think). We are not talking anything like the big twisters that wreak
havoc in the Caribbean and along tornado alley in the USA, but there
were trees falling on cars, and huge pieces of hoarding being tossed
about. Because we were on the Ridgeway, we were quite high up. We
were also on the second floor, so we could look out over Surrey. We
could see for miles. On that day, we could see nothing as all the street
lights were out. It was quite eerie. One of the chimneys in our block
was blown over and went through the building into a child's bedroom.
No injuries were caused thankfully, but the builders were there in days
chopping down the chimney stacks to below the level of the roofs. They
were only there for show anyway. Real fires hadn't been used in those
buildings for decades.

The only other incident there in the seven years that I was there was
a strange woman who appeared to be trying to bring the children into
her confidence. The oldest child there was about eight, and it was all a
little odd. We stepped up our vigilance and was ready to confront her
to find out what she was all about as soon as she revealed herself. She
never did, and the problem fizzled out.

We were finally encouraged to leave and find our own places to live.
The Met. was selling off its real estate to save money. What they gained
in selling them outstripped what they have now lost. I gather they
sold them cheaply. I have always felt uncomfortable about that. There
seems to be no logical honest reason to do this, and I sometimes wonder
which civil servant gained out of the sales. It may sound that I am a

little cynical, but I have no other explanation. While politicians were running around trying to root out corruption among the constables and sergeants, the real corruption was probably happening much higher up the food chain and was probably even more grubby on the civilian side of the services because there was little in the way of cheques and balances within the admin hierarchy.

So I no longer lived there. The Hand in Hand Public House, the Crooked Billet, the Rose and the Brewery Tap no longer enjoy my custom. I own my very own mortgage now, which is not a bad thing. At least I won't be hoiked out onto my ageing backside when I retire, which is what would have happened had I stayed in accommodation. I am not exactly landed gentry, but I am the king of my modest little castle.

The flats have gone now. They were pulled down and some plush flats built in its place. Each flat is now worth round about what the developers paid for the entire plot of land. I lived there in leafy Wimbledon and worked in slightly less leafy, but equally as plush, Chelsea—another very well-off area, and so my police career was launched without fanfare. We were earning decent money for the first time in our lives.

I wouldn't say that I made any lasting friendships from my time at Chelsea. I have not maintained contact with any of the families that I met there, but when I do come across any of them, which I do from time to time, it is always a pleasure and we have much to talk about. It is more like colleagues/acquaintances with whom I am friendly. My kids have formed lasting friendships from our time there. Some friendships were even formed indirectly and last to this day. I find great pleasure from this, as I never had the opportunity to form lifetime friendships from preschool times.

MONEY

I am not going to bang on about this too much. I am one of the least acquisitive people I know. I will never be rich because I never have the urge to do 'whatever it takes'. I seldom do the lottery, and I am never dreaming up schemes for the next million. I leave that to my brother. Money is necessary though, and police pay always looms large in our lives. There may be many reasons why people become police officers, but money is not one of them.

Years before I became a police officer, the government of the time decided that police were not earning a living wage,. And they were definitely not. It was late seventies. There was a Labour government in power, although they were in deep trouble. They had come to the conclusion that they needed the police. A huge reform of police pay was on the cards, and this came to fruition within the life of that parliament.

They started with raising the pay of all police officers. They then set overtime rates that protected police while, at the same time, allowing them to call us to duty when they needed us. They then put in place year-on-year increments of 1/2 per cent over the rate of inflation or 3.25 per cent whichever was highest. This was a generous package. It was mitigated a little by giving us some of the money in allowances. This allowed them to treat all the money we earned as taxable and pensionable, but part of our pay wouldn't enter into calculations when it came to such things as overtime. There was, of course, a payoff. In return for this, we had to agree to relinquish our right to take industrial action.

They made a differentiation between employees and office holders. Employees could strike, but could be made redundant. Office holders couldn't. This meant that as long as you kept your nose clean, you could keep your job for thirty plus years. We started paying into a very good pension scheme. It must have been good, the civil service had the same one—except that they didn't have to pay anything into theirs, and we had to pay 11 per cent of our salary into the scheme (this increased to 14.25 per cent later on). They then started a massive recruitment drive. By the time I joined, it was said that there were more graduates in the Met than any other organisation in the country. This was partly to do with massive unemployment, and partly to do with decent pay and conditions and promotion prospects.

I feel certain that with these conditions, the police were able to remain one of the least corrupt in the world. You will always get greedy idiots who will try to push the boundaries. There are enough ex-police contemplating their navels in prison to prove this point. The fact is that I have never witnessed anyone taking a bung. I have been offered a gratuity and politely declined. The vast majority of police will not go down the road of bribery. No one could afford the sort of sums that would outstrip the pension benefits and pay that we earn, certainly not for the sort of low-level information that they hold. I am not saying that we are rolling in it, but most police were able to own their own homes now, so we couldn't have been doing that badly. The police officer of the 1970s would not have been able to contemplate owning property without some sort of extra help.

When I joined, the service owned real estate and housed most of its police officers. The reason why they did this was so they could post us wherever they needed us. If we lived too far away, they could just simply move us to a different flat. This seldom happened, but they could do it. Police were allowed to own their own homes, but they had to buy houses within twenty-five miles of the centre of London. They also had to be able to guarantee that they could report for duty anywhere in the Met at any given time of day.

Money then started running out, and the police had to make savings. One way in which they decided to achieve this was to sell off their real estate. To do this, they had to encourage people to buy their own homes. They were getting free housing, and they were not going to be easy to shift. They offered a rent allowance for all those wishing to rent privately or buy. They then sold everything at knock-down prices. In due course, house prices outstripped the means of most police officers, particularly if they were first-time buyers. They tried recruiting from those people who already lived in London. This would, in theory, mean they already had somewhere to live. Unfortunately, they couldn't find enough people to recruit, so they abandoned that idea.

They then allowed police to buy from further afield. Now, of course, you have a situation that not all police officers can guarantee being able to get to anywhere in the Met at any given time because they were living 50, 60, or even 70 miles outside London. All the real estate was sold, so they had nowhere to put people. They even negotiated a deal to allow police to travel on British Rail for a relatively nominal sum to enable people to get in. The payoff there was that if there were any incidents on the train, they would be expected to deal with it. Most police probably would anyway, so the deal was done.

As the money in the government coffers shrank, more savings have to be made. The agreement that we came to in the seventies about not striking was ensconced in law. It is now illegal for police officers to take, or even contemplate, any form of industrial action. The government's side of the bargain remained an 'agreement' that they could ignore whenever they liked. By the end of Gordon Brown's time in office, they decided that they liked to ignore their side of the agreement and did. Pay started being reduced, pensions started to be threatened, allowances were taken away, and the protection afforded by the overtime agreement was stripped. At least the government had managed to keep the no-strike deal. It appears now that they want to have all the benefits afforded by us being so-called 'officers holders' (no industrial action, no lunch breaks, etc. while treating us like 'employees' with all the advantages that they can take out of that. Being able to make police officers redundant being one example).

It has got to the situation that they have to save money, but they keep telling people that they won't reduce numbers. How can they do this? Easy. Brand new police officers are half the price of experienced officers. Experience is, as far as those holding the purse strings are concerned, overrated. As I write this, no decisions have been made, but the writing is on the wall. The proposals on the table are to introduce a system where people are recruited at inspector and superintendent level. Constables will have little room for advancement up the ladder. Those who have to make life-changing decisions in respect of ordinary people will have no experience. Constables will have no senior officers to teach them how to be police officers.

Constables learn everything they know from going out there and doing the job. Sergeants are able to supervise the constables because they have done the same thing and know what needs to be done. Everyone in the police has started at constable level. That is why the system works. A sergeant does not gain his rank by passing an exam and taking promotion. He learns the job of constable, proves himself able, and uses his knowledge to pass an exam and then his assessment that gains him his rank. Inspectors, in the same way, don't just turn up, pass an exam, and start running murder investigations. One goes through the same process of constable, the sergeant, then an exam. An assessment of his/her abilities is then carried out, and he is promoted.

The whole process from starting out in Hendon to becoming an inspector takes years. There may well be people out there that can do the job without going through this process—people who have natural abilities. There are certainly inspectors who have been through the process who don't know their arse from their elbow. The job of an inspector is not an academic one. The best inspectors do not necessarily come from academic backgrounds. They are practical people who need to make good, clear decisions quickly and then stand by them. Some bloke who has done a theology degree and then gone on to be a department manager in a clothing chain is going to struggle.

Police officers spend their working lives learning how to control situations and the people involved in those situations. How does one turn up with no experience at all and try to control the controllers?

The Hillsborough disaster is being spoken about a lot. Much of what the media are saying is rubbish. There is, however, no doubt that the police operation was poorly thought out. Everyone is quick to blame the superintendent who was in charge of the operation. They are quick to tell everyone that he was inexperienced. Why do the government officials think that recruiting officers at superintendent level is then a good idea when inexperience can cause such disaster? Maybe it's because they are politicians, and my view on that bunch is not particularly charitable. They are right up there with lawyers, burglars, and fraudsters as far as dishonesty is concerned. Glad I am retiring soon.

My First Steps in the Real World

Chelsea was my first nick. This meant Harrods, Harvey Nichols, The Natural History, science, and V&A Museums. It is a strange area. Very wealthy and very poor living in close proximity with very little in between. It is only about 1.5² miles. It is the last place in the world to which I would ascribe the phrase 'real world'. In that small area, there are about five council estates housing the poorest people living cheek by jowl with celebrities and the wealthy. People who couldn't afford cars living next to families that were buying Jaguars for their darling little 17-year-old sons and daughters to learn to drive in. It has always been an arty area. You just have to look at the street and building names like Holbein Square, Whistler Walk, Gunter Grove, among others.

Turner, the artist, lived there, as did A. A. Milne and Arthur Conan Doyle. I learned to be able to pitch myself to whoever I was dealing with easily. A little burglar isn't going to have any respect for you if you start calling him sir and speaking to him politely. I am not one to use expletives much, but your average villain knows very little else. You have to go to their level. Throw in a few *F*s and *C*s if absolutely necessary. I did this on only a very few occasions, as I really don't swear, and it doesn't trip off my tongue very easily. I felt self-conscious and was sure that person I was dealing with would suss it out, and I would lose the exchange. 'Good afternoon, sir, and how are you this fine day?' is going to get you nowhere. 'You all right, mate? What you up to? Got anything on you that you shouldn't have?' will get to either 'No, officer, I ain't got nuffin. Look, you can check.' Or it will get you abuse, but that will be because he is probably carrying something he shouldn't have. You wouldn't want to talk in that manner to other residents like Sir David Frost or Felicity Kendall.

We always had to treat everyone with a certain amount of respect regardless of who they were because there were all sorts of judges and barristers and MPs living there. You just never knew who you were going to encounter, or who was watching you dealing with Billy Burglar. There were other challenges to working there. Chelsea just was not a very busy place to work as a police officer. There were loads of people with influence, so there were always plenty of police around. We just didn't have much to do. In the busier places like Brixton and Croydon, police are tearing around from one crisis to another. They don't have time for anything. In Chelsea, we were tripping over each other. A bored police officer is not a good one. There was a lot a bickering and backstabbing because they had too much time on their hands. There are very few people who I have kept in touch with because of that.

A CULTURE-FREE CANTEEN

There was a lot said about canteen culture. In actual fact, police canteens and Petri dishes have been unfavourably compared, and it appears that that you *can* develop a culture on a Petri dish! Unfortunately, this is not the same for the canteen. People imagine canteen culture as police getting together and scheming about how to stitch innocent people up. This is rubbish. Police do not lose or gain anything by trying to stitch innocent people up. There is no point. I never witnessed anything outrageous like it in my entire career.

I remember one officer that I spoke to once. He is no longer a police officer, but he told me that he had been carrying a very large knife around with him for a fortnight. He had stopped a well-known thief two weeks previous. He had searched him and found nothing. When the man walked away, the officer noticed something in the gutter close to where he had first spotted the man. It was a French loaf inside of which was the knife. He had been had over by the man he had stopped, and he wanted to 'give' it back in such a way that he could arrest him for the possession of the offensive weapon. He gave up after two weeks, thankfully. I was not comfortable with what he was planning. My attitude is that these people will come again. We will always catch them doing something wrong and prosecute them legitimately. The thing is that he did not advertise what he was doing. No one knew, including me, while it was going on. Don't get me wrong, I don't deny that there are police officers out there who are bent, but they are mercifully few, and they don't show out—certainly not in a canteen.

I like to tell people that 85 per cent of working police officers will admit to having been had over by someone in their career, the other 15 per cent are lying. There was, of course, a canteen culture of sorts, but this was more to do with pecking orders, hierarchy, and cliques—the sort of stuff that I turned my nose up at. You had the 'driver's table' where only officers who were qualified to drive police cars could sit. You had young probationary PCs, fresh out of Hendon, being ignored and told to go sit on another table. The advanced driver was top Johnny Banana, and everyone deferred to him. I say 'him', as there were precious few female advanced drivers at that time. This, to me, was intolerable (that is, the canteen culture, not the dearth of female drivers. I didn't know better then).

Most of my contemporaries were nineteen or twenty and had seen nothing of life. I was twenty-six. That was quite old for a new police officer in the late eighties. The problem was that I had seen a bit of life, and I was not impressed by who could and who couldn't drive. I wasn't going to be treated as a second-class citizen by some snotty-nosed, wet-behind-the-ears copper just because he had been doing the job for eighteen months longer than I had.

We would go to the pub after late turns sometimes. It was expected that the probby (probationary constable—what we used to be called while we were going through our two years of probationary period) would buy the advanced driver a pint. I had no problem with this if he returned the compliment. As a consequence of all this, I was not the most popular guy on the block. I didn't toe the line! They couldn't fault me for my work ethic, but they didn't have to put me forward for the better jobs either. The problem with me is that I am bloody-minded, and I would not give up. This is probably a throwback from my days growing up in Zimbabwe, not being subject to the peer pressure of taking drugs or doing anything unless I wanted to.

THE NUT JOB

A time came when I could get a driving course. I had been overlooked a couple of times and hadn't said anything or asked why, but I couldn't just keep rolling over. A driving course meant that you would not have to be stuck in the station office and custody suite, so it was a good course to have. The driving school was also world-renowned as a centre of excellence, so the course was sought after. I eventually approached my inspector and said to him that I would like to know why I was being overlooked. If I was doing something wrong, I could rectify it. He had never suggested that I was not doing what I should. I think I backed him into a corner. It was a question he couldn't easily answer. Instead of being honest and say that he wanted someone else, as he had no faith in me, he took a different tack. He essentially suggested that I had a psychological issue and referred me to a psychologist.

I was visited at home by some people who asked me a number of questions. They then went onto the subject of alcohol. I told them quite truthfully that I had a bottle of whisky in the kitchen. 'How long have you had that bottle?'

'About six months,' said I, again, perfectly truthfully. The bottle was still half-full.

I like a sip of whisky every now and again. The interview was very quickly wound up, and they left. It was only when I was going through this with the psychologist that I realised that my inspector was basically accusing me of being an alcoholic. I have always been a bit dizzy, and my diction has always been a little slurred. I am also terrible at leaving things lying around and misplacing things. He clearly chose to believe that this was a symptom of a drinking problem. He failed to get me on the alcoholism, as I simply was not.

We went to the next phase—the psychologist. I arrived at the place nice and early and we went through the process. I wasn't aware that I was being analysed from before I even arrived. The fact that I was thirty minutes early, and I was well turned out, everything went into the mix. I came out of there with a very good bill of mental health, a more than respectable IQ, and a short-term memory off the scale. I returned to work and informed my inspector, who said that these tests can be manipulated, and ignored everything. I think he was trying to give me the tin tack. He could not do that on my performance, so he tried by trying to trash my character. He failed dismally, and I continued. I kept rubbing him up the wrong way by doing everything correctly, so he couldn't get me on anything. An excellent way to learn the job, and I have that tosser to thank for it.

I got my driving course, as he had nowhere else to turn. It was a good course. I would recommend anyone to take an extra driving course after they have been driving for a couple of years. It can only help. As far as driving for the police is concerned, the excitement wears off very quickly. I will personally never drive a marked police car in anger again. There are all sorts of stupid performance indicators, which mean that inspectors expect you to get to calls five minutes before you are called to go to it. They expect you to do the lot, but if you have an accident getting to the call, they throw the book at you. They regularly send police officers to court for dangerous driving *because* you were on a blue light run, not because you were dangerous. This means that your own personal licence is endorsed or even taken away from you. The attitude appears to be that the police service is doing *me* a favour by allowing me to drive their cars. My attitude is that I will do them a favour by driving their cars if, and only if, they supported me when an accident happens that is not my fault. Until that day, I will not do it. Therefore, I will never do it because that day will never happen.

Not on My Watch

It is the same for firearms. As I write this, I am aware that two female police officers have been lured to the premises of a person ostensibly to report a burglary. They were shot dead by some vicious scumbag on their arrival. This has reopened the debate about police carrying firearms. In my view, there is no debate. I will not carry a firearm on duty in this police service. The government coffers are not rich enough to afford to pay me enough to do so. There are firearms-trained officers. They have a clear mandate, and they have clear protocols. They cannot produce their firearms unless there is a life-and-death situation. They cannot discharge their firearms unless they believe that the person who they are aiming at is going to endanger someone's life there and then.

On the rare occasion that happens, the officer who uses his gun is suspended and effectively investigated for murder. These are people who want to protect life and who risk their own to do it. They are thanked by being accused of murder. No thank you. It will never happen to me. Even if the media wound their collective necks in and supported us a little, but they are only after bad news, and there is nothing better for them than to be whisked along on the media bandwagon to string police officers up when they are perceived to have stepped over the line. It is too high a price to pay for trying to protect our community.

To Catch a Thief

There were some interesting interludes during my time there. We once decided to do an operation to try to catch handbag thieves. It all seems quite low-level, but handbag thieves are specialists in their own field. They tend to stick to what they know best, and they seem to be very similar in many aspects. When we set-up the operation, we started by doing some basic number crunching. How many handbags were being stolen, how often, how many and where were they being taken from.

We were quite surprised at our results. We found that roughly one-third were being stolen around the Knightsbridge area, one-third in the immediate surroundings of Sloane Square, and the other one-third were going from the rest of Chelsea. Knightsbridge was difficult, as the incidents were spread throughout several shops, two of which had their own store detectives. Obviously, the latter one-third would be very hit and miss. Sloane Square, on the other hand, was very small, and the incidents were going from three different premises. The big department store, Peter Jones, had its own security. The second was a busy pub and the third was a wine bar. About 1/3 of all incidents were occurring in this wine bar, and it was happening most days, so we were bound to find something.

The next thing we studied were the thieves themselves. For this, we brought in a colleague who had been looking at the problem for some time and had an excellent talk arranged. In essence, he told us that all handbag thieves were feeding drug habits. They needed cash fast. They all went into premises that were likely to have plenty of cash and cards. To do this, they had to look respectable. Unfortunately, they spent most of their money on drugs, so they couldn't afford much. The result was that they would generally look respectable from a distance but would not bear close inspection. Then they would need something that would conceal their ill-gotten gains. A coat over their forearm would be the normal sort of thing. As they were working and not particularly interested in drinking, they would not be buying large amounts of alcohol. They had to blend in though, so a half pint or a small bottle would be their thing. They would then wander around. Finally, we were told that once stopped by police, if they think they had a chance, they would run; but once caught, provided that you were reasonable with them, they would reciprocate.

The operation is then set-up. We also found in our research of CCTV footage that the thieves tended to overlook waiters. We spoke to the proprietor of the wine bar and put one chap in as a glass waiter. I went in there as a middle management type fellow with a younger, good-looking female colleague. Read into that what you wish. We were given clearance to drink alcohol in strict moderation. We went there and bought a bottle of wine and watched out. We nursed the wine for quite a while but eventually finished it.

We had no takers. I decided to have one more glass each, then we would call it a day. As I sat down with my glass, a man walked in. He was everything we had studied. Right down to the coat over the crook of his arm. I called the 'waiter', and got him to keep an eye on him if he went out of our sight. He bought a small bottle of beer and started wandering around. He went downstairs. The glass waiter suddenly had an urge to collect glasses downstairs. Five minutes later, he came up. He was definitely looking, according to our tame waiter, but no takers. He then came back upstairs and walked to the end of the bar and out of sight again.

I had worked out that the female toilets were close to where he was, so I asked my colleague to go to the toilet and keep a surreptitious eye on him. She went to the toilet, then spent about one nanosecond in there before she came back to me almost at a sprint. As she had walked past, he was in the process of picking a pocket. He started walking towards us, and we stopped him at the exit to the bar. He immediately took off into the street, hotly pursued and rugby-tackled by me. Once secured, I made sure he was okay and that he wasn't hurt. He said that he was fine and that I would find what I was looking for in his back pocket.

ROLEX POLE AXED

A colleague and friend of mine were out in plain clothes over the period of a few days one summer when we noticed that a particular group of ne'er-do-wells were always hanging around at a particular bus stop. This was at a time when Rolex watch robberies were happening on a regular basis. You could see these thieves walking down the road asking people the time. A message would go up, and an identified victim would be followed off and robbed. We worked out that it was this group who were awaiting the signal. We set-up an operation to observe them and build up some evidence. Unfortunately, it was also at a time when we had to tell virtually everyone in the police service what we were doing. This was supposed to prevent us from bumbling into someone else's op. Sounds perfectly reasonable, but the problem comes when one of those police officers has their own agenda.

By the time we set-up, all the thieves had scattered, and we gathered not one jot of intelligence on Rolex watch robberies. We did gain intel on a dodgy chemist but nothing on Rolex watches. The op was declared unsuccessful, as we hadn't arrested anyone or gathered intelligence. They weren't interested that Rolex watch robberies dropped off in that area to virtually nothing and remained so until I left the division. Apparently, they can't accurately assess crime prevention, so they aren't interested. Of course, the general public knew nothing of it because they were not becoming victims anymore. I stick two fingers up to those bean pushers, and personally declare that operation successful because I did what our primary function is: to *prevent* crime!

PHASE 2

———■ ■———

Senior police officers (that is senior in terms of rank, not age) are only interested in one thing: the next rank, the climb up the greasy pole to the upper echelons. They do this by coming up with ideas that will change the course of history in their eyes. Most of these ideas are brilliant on paper. It is because most of these people are so removed from the cut and thrust of policing the frontline, they will never understand that ideas on paper seldom translate to street level. They also do not realise that most ideas have been thought of before. The police service has been going since 1829. It is arrogance of the highest order to think that any of their stupid ideas haven't been thought of before. The reason why they are not being used is because it didn't work on the first, second, and fifteenth time they were tried out by some airhead trying to find a route to the top job.

JUMP BEFORE THE PUSH

When I had been doing the job for ten years, the powers that be decided that anyone who had been in their role for ten years or more should be moved. The reason for this was that people tend to go off the boil after a while, and a change is the right way to reinvigorate their careers. Of course, they are not interested in the fact that some people really do enjoy what they are doing. They are enthusiastic in their role and function at a high level doing that role. Those people, and there were many, were hoiked out of the job that they had taken years building a high level of expertise and dumped onto the streets of an area that they had no knowledge of to walk the beat. Years of training down the drain at the stroke of a pen owned by someone who was one rank better off.

There are shed loads of police officers out there that are coasting. They are bored, uninterested, and just wait for the clock to strike five at the end of the day and their pay cheque at the end of each month. These officers need to be kicked up the bum and moved around until they find something that they enjoy doing and start being effective. All officers are annually assessed and this, one would think, is the ideal time to find those people and deal with them. The problem is that the assessment process makes it so difficult to mark anyone up or down that it becomes useless. If you are not very good at what you do and keep making mistakes, the sergeant is expected to highlight this in the assessment. He is also expected to show what he has done about it.

As a general rule, the honest answer is nothing, so the assessors just tell all that the officers is performing perfectly adequately. You then don't find anyone underperforming, and you, therefore, can't deal with them appropriately. At the same time, if someone is performing off the charts, they don't want to lose them, so they assess them in good—but not excellent—terms. This all means that everyone gets put into the bag, and everyone ends up getting transferred, good, bad, or indifferent.

So it was that I was rapidly approaching my ten years, so I pre-empted it all and put in for a move to South Norwood. I had never been to South Norwood. I didn't even know it existed before I put in for the transfer. It was actually only six miles from where I lived—a part of Croydon Borough and a world away from Chelsea.

I knew every inch of Chelsea. I walked the beat for six years and drove it for a further four years. There were few places I did not know about. There was no street untrodden by me. I didn't need a map. It was all upstairs locked in my fuzzy brain. South Norwood was far too big to deal with. It stretched from Streatham Common to the southern reaches of Addington, a distance of ten miles. From Coulsdon and Sutton to West Wickham, a distance of around five or six miles,

Chelsea was 1.5^2 miles. Officers who had been there for years still needed a map book to navigate their way around. No one walked the beat; it was just too big.

The people were different too. I dealt with one domestic incident all the time I was in Chelsea. We were dealing with them every day in South Norwood. Gangs roamed the streets. Police officers were few and far between. There were fewer officers in that area than in Chelsea, and they had further to go when you were in trouble. Some of my colleagues actually tested it out one night at about 4 a.m. They did a blue light run from the northernmost point to the southernmost point. There was no traffic, and it was a free run. It took them twelve minutes. It doesn't seem much, but when you are being attacked, seconds are of the essence. Twelve minutes is a lifetime.

It was a busy police area. This was a good thing. Busy people do not have time to bitch and moan about nothing and everything, they just get on with it. On the other hand, things don't get done as thoroughly because you are always under pressure to get to the next call. This was my first taste of going into houses where you would wipe your feet on the way out! There were no shops wanting us to go in there and have a cup of coffee, as a way of deterring the young thugs that hung around. I took months to get used to reporting burglaries where the only thing that was stolen was a £50 TV. I had been used to reporting burglaries where the amounts went into tens of thousands. Why would anyone bother with an old TV?

It was also the first time I had seen anywhere like Addington—commonly referred to as Adders or the Addo. I was told when I went there that there were more convicted criminals per capita in Addington than anywhere in Europe. These were people who didn't report burglaries. If they had been burgled, they would find out who it was and sort it all out themselves. No need for the Old Bill to snoop around in their business. There were obviously many families that were normal ordinary law-abiding citizens, but you seldom interacted with them.

OVER TO THE DARK SIDE

After a couple of years, I started realising that I needed to do something else. My career was going nowhere. I was not getting the sort of stimulation that I needed. I decided to try the investigation side of my job: the CID, referred to as the dark side by my uniformed colleagues. In those days, the uniformed guys had to deal with most of the stuff they came across. The CID was an investigative unit. They dealt with the more complex investigations and left relatively minor stuff to the arresting officers. What this meant was that young uniformed officers gained experience of evidential criteria.

In the brave world, in which I now operate, things have changed. Everything is compartmentalised. Uniformed officers are called to an incident, they report it, and if there is a suspect on hand, they arrest. They then take them back to a police station and hand over the lot to a trainee detective. Detectives then get stuck dealing with petty offences. They don't get sufficient time to deal properly with the more serious offences; mistakes are made, cases are lost. In the meantime, the uniformed officers are being deskilled. They do not learn the evidential reasons for doing things, so things are overlooked. This, in my humble opinion, is a disastrous policy. Nothing good comes out of officers who are not allowed to gain experience. Thankfully, I had that knowledge of twelve years of dealing with offences, processing prisoners, and taking minor offences to court.

I started in the newly formed Community Safety Unit (CSU), which was just what they called the unit that dealt with domestic assaults. Having dealt with one domestic incident in the entire time I worked at Chelsea, I had only the previous two years experience to fall back on. South Norwood was full of people who seemed to marry people who they hated. It was full on. It just kept coming at you. There were no hiding places. Domestic argument after domestic argument after domestic assault, it just went on.

DRUGS OR PROSTITUTION, YOUR CHOICE

None of this prepared me for my first real brush with the other side. Intelligence came to light that someone, with whom I had a very brief encounter, wanted to try to stitch me up and get me and a colleague to lose our jobs. He was an ex-fireman who was stalking an ex-girlfriend. He was obsessive and could not leave her alone. He was investigated by my colleague before I even joined the unit. The result was that he was charged under the Prevention From Harassment Act. He was found guilty and given a restraining order preventing him from making contact with the woman in question. He broke the terms of the restraining order almost immediately. He was again investigated, and as a result of that investigation, police decided to charge him. This is where I step in. I was simply asked to be there when he was charged. I said nothing to him. I dealt with him quickly and bailed him to court.

Obviously, because my name was on the charge sheet and my colleague's name was there as the investigating officer, he took it upon himself to get revenge on the only two names he had. He had recently left the fire service and had a load of cash as a result. He wanted to get us into trouble. He wasn't worried about what sort of trouble, although he quite liked the idea of either drugs or prostitution or both. I had a little giggle over this. There is nothing that could have lured me into either of those areas.

In the event, the police service put a number of protective bits in place. In the meantime, an undercover officer was sent in to try to get to the bottom of it. After a week, I was informed that he had gone as far as negotiating a deal. Unfortunately, he had fallen into a serious cocaine habit and blown all his money. It all fizzled out because he simply couldn't afford it. I never really worried about any of it. If his intention was to lure me into breaking the law, he would have to wake up early in the morning to get past me.

The Question Is

One of my aims from very early on in my role as an investigator was to improve my interview techniques. With the advent of tape-recorded interviews and new legislation limiting, or at least placing a caveat on people's right to silence, we had to interview more people. Detained people did not have to answer any of our questions. This has never been taken away as a right. What was removed was the idea that someone could refuse to answer questions, get together with their mates, work out a story, then go to court, and tell the world that they had an alibi.

Essentially, it meant that if you chose not to answer questions in the first place, then the court could draw an inference as to their honesty if they then came up with an account later on. If they did not do it and were not there at the time, then why not tell the police in the first instance and save the taxpayer another court case? Of course, if you are innocent, most people would want to shout it from the rooftops straight away. The legislation also prevented them from changing their account without consequences.

It was also considered when the Police and Criminal Evidence (PACE) Act first came out that as soon as police had sufficient evidence to charge someone, they should stop the interview and either charge, caution, or release. The problem with that was that the defendants were coming up with accounts at court, and they were being found not guilty. It was felt that if they had been given the opportunity to have their say in the first place, the time and expense of a court case would be spared. It was therefore decided that we should interview people in most cases, whether they had sufficient evidence or not, if only to give the defendant his opportunity. Interviews then became commonplace. New techniques had to be learned. Solicitors were figuring out ways of throwing spanners into the works.

Silence is Golden

'No comment' interviews are still commonplace, and we have our ways of dealing with them. I have only ever had one occasion where the person I was interviewing said nothing at all. Most people give a little smirk and say, 'No comment.' But at least they give their name for the benefit of the tape. This man, who was arrested for a domestic assault again, said absolutely nothing at all. He didn't want a solicitor. I was on my own, as everyone else was busy. He would not stop talking, as he was being booked in. As we went into the interview room, the verbal diarrhoea was never-ending. He just would not stop.

I undid the seals on some fresh tapes and put them into the machine in his presence. Natter, natter, natter, on and on it went. I then turned on the tape recorder . . . Nothing! Absolute silence! He did not sniff, burp, or scratch his backside, nothing! If anyone were to listen to the tape recording, they would find no evidence of anyone other than me in the interview room. There was no CCTV in custody suites in those days. Because they are given this opportunity to have their say, and they are told that if they were asked similar questions at court and they answered the questions that they previously didn't answer, the courts could take a dim view—this meant that we would have to carry on asking questions even when they don't answer. It was really odd asking a question, waiting a few seconds, and then asking another with silence in between—very unnatural. The interview lasted about ten minutes, and I turned the tapes off. It was at this point that the verbal floodgates opened once again. He walked away unscathed in the end because, as usual, the victim wouldn't substantiate.

A QUICK IN-AND-OUT

In today's brave new world, we are ruled by gigabytes and cyberphiles. It used to take two to three hours to deal with a shoplifter. That would mean going to the shop, arresting, taking him to the police station, booking him in, taking fingerprints, getting a statement from the shop owner, charging, and completing the paperwork. Nowadays, it takes two hours before you even get to speak to a custody officer. You are looking a minimum of six hours just to book them in, interview, and release on bail. If you are looking at charging someone, you can double that.

Despite that, I still managed to arrest someone, book him in, interview, charge, take him to court, and have him convicted in 1 ¾ hours! This was an odious man who was well known in the area. He was paraplegic and swanned around annoying as many people as he could in his electric wheelchair. Inevitably, a woman came along thinking she could change his dastardly ways. And also inevitably, she failed spectacularly. He started stalking her and was dealt with for harassment. A restraining order was the decision of the learned magistrate. He was never going to take that seriously, and within hours, he was back in his wheelchair outside her house shouting and swearing and just being everything he was known to be.

She contacted me, and I gathered the evidence and sent out the word that he was to be arrested. Before long, I heard that he had been spotted. He was hoisted into the back of a van—wheelchair and all—and carted to the station. The custody officer took one look and immediately started working out ways of getting him out. He knew all his details, so he didn't need to have him sitting there while he was booked in. He heard the evidence to satisfy himself that the arrest was lawful and told him his rights. He didn't want a solicitor, so the custody officer suggested that I interview him while he booked him in.

The interview lasted fifteen minutes by which time the custody officer had completed what he had to do. I put the case to him along with the restraining order, and he agreed that he should be charged. It was 1.30 p.m. by this time, and the custody officer drew up the charges. But not before he had contacted the court, which was a five-minute walk away, and confirmed that they could deal with his straight away. He was duly charged, and I then walked him to the court. We went into court, one where the clerk read out the charges and asked how he pleaded. He pleaded guilty and was punished there and then. Isn't it amazing what people can do when they concentrate?

HE'S THE GEEZER WHAT DONE IT

Identification issues are something that coppers fall foul of regularly. Not because they are not able to identify the suspect.

It is more a case of not being able to plug every hole, no matter how insignificant, to the satisfaction of the defence. No longer is it just a case of the aggrieved person pointing a finger and saying, 'He's the geezer what done it. I saw it with my own eyes!' That would be far too easy, and some poor, bedraggled solicitor will go home unable to put food on the table if we were to do the easy thing. Even if someone was to say, 'It was my next-door neighbour. The one who lives in the house immediately to the left. He lives on his own. He's a crotchety, old bugger, and I saw him do it. I don't know what his name is, but it was him.' A statement like that would get the ID police out in force.

There are several ways of achieving ID. If a woman says, 'It was my husband,' that is quite clear unless she is a bigamist, but that will be for another day. If police saw it and interrupted whatever was happening there and then, and arrested the villain, that would be clear. If, however, someone walked up to a copper and told him that he was walking down the road minding his own business when this bloke came up to him and smacked him in the face, breaking his nose. The police officer would hopefully notice that he has the requisite broken nose and start asking questions. 'How long ago?' 'Five minutes, officer.' 'Which way did he go?' 'That-a-way, officer.' 'What did he look like?' And a description is given. This is where it all starts falling down.

Even at this early stage, what the officer *has* to do is record the first description there and then. They even have a section in their pocketbooks with body maps and everything. How often is this used? Seldom! How often do we lose a case because we have not properly recorded events? Regularly. Having established an offence has occurred and that there is a nasty on the loose possibly breaking every nose he can find. They put him in the back of a police car and drove him around. Now, we can't go around saying, 'Was it him? What about him and that geezer over there?' That would be coaching. You can point to a general group and say, 'Can you see anyone in there who matches the description?' Sometimes, he spots the guy and points him out. Again, we record his exact words. There is a world of difference between 'that looks a bit like him' or 'I think it was him' and 'that's the bloke, he did it, no doubt whatsoever'. What should then happen is that another officer is sent in to confront and probably arrest, while the victim is taken away to make a statement.

You may think job done, but no. It's just started. Before I go into that, we can look at a slightly adjusted scenario. The victim has given a description of a bloke wearing a bright orange T-shirt and torn jeans. While he is talking to the police, the description is going out over the airwaves. Officers stop a man in that exact clothing, complete with blood splatters, and in the right area walking in the right direction. The correct procedure is to arrest straight away and ensure that the victim does not see him. The description is enough when it is that distinctive. I have seen police bring the victim to have a look at him to confirm that they have the right man. Wrong, wrong, wrong. In both of these cases, a formal ID procedure—what used to be called an ID parade—needs to be started up. As soon as the victim sees the suspect before this is put into place, the ID is corrupted, and you lose your case there and then. It doesn't matter that they have the right man or anything like that. You have screwed up the ID procedure, and that is enough.

If all this initial identification stuff comes to nought, we can show the person photographs. There have to be at least twelve photos of different people to look at. This is not something we resort to often. If someone is picked out, we then have to move onto the ID parade. Any defence solicitor will claim that a positive identification is unsafe. They will argue that the victim picked out the wrong person when he saw the photos, and he was just picking out the guy he saw on the photos. It all becomes a bit pointless. There are plenty of other pointless rules like the investigating officer has to distance himself from the ID issues completely. There isn't any way he can influence them in any event, but he still has to stay away.

Anyway, where were we? Villain is trussed up and bundled unceremoniously into the police station where he is interviewed. If he puts himself on the scene involved in a fracas with our victim, then ID is no longer an issue. If, however, he denies all or doesn't answer any questions, then ID is still to be sorted out. Instead of having eight elderly white little old men lining up with an 18-year-old black youth so that the victim cannot be mistaken about who he picks out, we go down a more techno route. Of course, we never did that. We always tried to get similar looking people in for the line-up.

Now, we do it all on video. Some wise guy judge back in the nineties decided, for reasons best known to himself, that for an identification to be successful, the victim only had to identify that facial features. It seems no one told him that people can be recognised using all sorts of other features: height, build, hair colour, gait, etc. So now, everyone is filmed from the shoulder up and has to provide front and profile views. Eight other similar people are then downloaded onto nine discs, all with the suspect in different position within the parade. The victim can then come along once the suspect is out of sight, pick one disc, and see if he can recognise the face of the suspect. If he is not picked out, that is the end of the job normally. It doesn't matter how sure you are, once ID becomes an issue, the case will normally live or die on the back of it. If, on the other hand, the suspect is picked out, the solicitors get to work on trashing that evidence on procedure alone because there are so many pitfalls.

I was investigating a very nasty, racially aggravated GBH. The victim was Asian, and the suspects were mixed-race Caribbean. We managed to catch one guy quickly and charged him. The second guy proved much more elusive. We had arrested someone and arranged an ID parade, but in the meantime, I had to resort to the photograph albums for the last suspect. He managed to pick out the guy quite easily. He had seen him in his local area several times, so he was in no doubt who he was. He was arrested and no commented everything and ID procedures were put in place. A few days later, I took the victim to view the ID line-up for the second guy. He didn't pick any one out. I drove him back home, and as we were arriving in his road, he saw the third guy walking in the road. He recognised him from behind (so much for facial features), but I confirmed it was the same guy he had identified in the photos as we drove passed. I took a statement and thought to myself, *Job done.*

What's the point of ID procedure? He has identified the man. Even if this wasn't good enough—and I could see no reason why it wasn't— the integrity of the ID issues was damaged. A week later, we went to court to deal with the first guy. As we got there, the first guy was talking to the second and third guy in court. The victim once again spotted him immediately. A statement was once again taken. This guy has now been identified three times and has been linked to the other suspect. There was no doubt that I had the right man. He was charged, and it went to the crown court where the case was thrown out due to unsafe identification—go figure. All this was at a time when they were changing and refining ID procedures, and they appeared to think it necessary to backdate everything to a time before the start of the offence the was committed. A very complicated way of getting someone to say, 'He's the geezer what done it,' and making it stick.

DETECTIVE INSPECTORS

———— ■ ● ■ ————

As is my wont, I managed to continue to wind up the wrong people throughout my time—the DIs! As the poster on my bedroom wall said when I was 15, 'A disagreeable person is someone who disagrees with me.' Most DIs would fall into this mantra. Don't get me wrong, there were many with whom I got along well. With those DIs, I had a very good working relationship. Having established myself in the role of detective, I found that I wasn't bad at it. It didn't take long before other DCs and trainee DCs were bypassing sergeants and inspectors to come to me for advice. I made no bones about what I did and didn't know. If I didn't know it, I would help them find the answer. If I did, I made sure they understood. I always found it pointless to just give someone an answer then walk away. That way, no one learned anything. Demonstrations and examples were always more helpful. I found it difficult, throughout my life, to accept incomplete or generalised answers. It suggested to me that the person either didn't know the answer and wasn't prepared to admit it or they just couldn't be bothered.

One of the problems that started immerging after a while was the fact that most DIs in Croydon (South Norwood had, by this time, joined forces with Croydon) were all uniformed officers who had never investigated anything and had transferred across after they had been promoted to inspector. The job of the uniformed inspector and the DI are vastly different. Uniformed inspectors deal with inexperienced officers, low-level crimes, and custody issues. DIs oversee higher level investigations and deal with more experienced officers. The decision-making processes are different in each case. There are more rules and regulations that we are subject to every day of our lives when dealing with detainees and everyone else. It is all very well learning it from a book, but you never understand it all until it is put into practise. If you never actually put it into practise, then you will struggle to argue points of law with those of the lower ranks who do it every day.

Let me regale you with some of my more memorable dealings with those who were two ranks above me. If you think about it, these are only a few examples in a long career. This simply means that either I was doing it right all the other times or the supervisors were not making a big deal about it. Let me reiterate that most of my dealings were very positive. These examples were not they!

If They Don't Get Me Coming

My first DI started well. He was a career detective and really did know what he was talking about. I was brand new in the investigating game, and he noticed that I was going off in the wrong direction in one of my first investigations. If I carried on, I would have found myself in problems. Most DIs would either not even know there was a problem or they would just not be interested and would have waited until I hung myself, so they could throw my carcase to the wolves. This DI took me into his office and told me what was wrong and what I should do to make it right. He told me not to worry about what had happened up until then. He would take the flak for that. A very decent gesture, and I learned quickly.

There came a point, however, that he started seeing one of the women in my unit. As is often the case, it all went wrong. They were both married to other people, and it blew up. The DI got into trouble with the DCI and was put on notice. He needed to take it out on someone, and I was the target. I was on my CID course (yes, we do have to learn how to be a tech). I got a telephone call by the DI wanting to know where a CCTV tape was. Of course, I didn't know off the top of my head, and I told him so. He took it upon himself to search my desk and found the tape sealed in an evidence secure bag. I can't remember why he needed it so desperately, but he lost all sense of perception. He dragged me into the office, gave me an addressing down, served me with an official form reporting me for something or other, and hoofed me out of the robbery squad that I had been working at for thirty days. I was put in a unit that dealt with the lowest level crime and had to be closely supervised.

Fortunately, the person doing the supervising had worked with me before and had no problem with my abilities. The form that I was served with meant that I would be disciplined by the superintendent. I carried on doing what I did and showing that I could do the job. Six months later, I told my supervisor that I had heard nothing about the disciplinary aspect. She was not happy with this and investigated. She found that the superintendent had—rather ironically—put it in his drawer and forgotten about it. They had to abandon the issue.

Not satisfied with this, my new DI wanted to do something and so kept me where I was. About six months earlier, I had dealt with an incident that involved someone waving a firearm out of a red car. This was all the information I had to go on. No type of car, no registration number, no description of car or youths, nothing. I went to a local petrol station to check the CCTV. I took the tape back to the police station, checked the video, and found that there was no one on the footage at all. The camera was pointing in the wrong direction. I took the video back and closed the crime down. No leads to chase, no witnesses, nothing.

Nine months later, my telephone rings, and I speak to a colleague who asks me about the job. Of course, this was two hours of my life nine months previously. I had dealt with a multitude of incidents since. I had not a clue what he was talking about. He informed me that he was at court, and they wanted the footage for that incident. Apparently, the exact same thing happened a week after the one I dealt with and the youths were captured. My colleague dealt with it and included my investigation with his. By the time I was called, they had gone to trial, and they wanted the footage. I had to go to court and explain that I simply couldn't remember anything about the incident much less the location of the tapes. As a result of this, the court dropped both charges despite the fact that there was overwhelming evidence in the second incident.

As far as they were concerned, they needed to see the footage, and if they couldn't, the trial was forfeit. When my new DI got to hear about this, it was manna from heaven. When I had taken the video to the station, I should have booked it into property, signed it out to view it, booked it back in when finished, and then got the owner to sign for it when I returned it. As my investigation was dead in the water before it even started, I did what most detectives would do and avoided unnecessary paperwork. All very well until this happened. The DI was able to reissue the disciplinary form and deal with it properly. I admitted to a very minor issue, and they were happy. The world had not stopped revolving on its axis, and I was able to continue winding inspectors up.

Incidentally, the first DI spoke to me when I had finished my period of training and became a fully fledged tech. He said something about throwing a lot of hurdles in my way and was happy that I had negotiated them well. He essentially agreed—although not in so many words—that he had overreacted.

MONEY FOR OLD JEWELLERY

My next nemesis was and still is an idiot. By now, there was only one career detective in the DI ranks—the only one that did not know the first thing about investigation. I had dealt with an incident a number of years earlier. In short, a family, who didn't like their daughter's boyfriend, came to report that some jewellery was stolen. They had traced the jewellery to a pawnbroker and found their daughter's boyfriend's signature on the form. Proof positive, you might think. He was duly arrested and interviewed. He claimed that he had a brother who had visited them and probably stole it. He had a habit of forging his signature.

The account was absolutely rubbish, but it was going to be difficult to prove it. It was made even worse when the daughter came into the police station of her own volition and signed a statement saying that it was she who stole the jewellery and got her boyfriend to pawn it, thinking she owned it. This was more than plausible, as she would know where the property was to be found in the first place. The fact that it was in a sealed envelope was not a problem, as she knew what was there. I had left the property in the pawnbrokers, but as it was subject to investigation, they were not allowed to sell it or return it to anyone other than the owners.

I spoke to the victims and told them what happened. I informed them that I had to go where the evidence took me. If I was to prosecute the boyfriend, I had no choice but to prosecute their daughter too. If they didn't want their daughter prosecuted, I would have to drop the prosecution against the bloke. They weren't happy but would not prosecute their daughter. I then forgot about it. I thought that the daughter would buy the property back from the pawnbrokers or the parents would just swallow the expense and pay themselves. Two years later, I was called and asked about the property. I found that the pawnbrokers had legal rights over the property in most cases, so I would not be able to restore the property.

Anyway, I argued that all the daughter had to do if she had stolen it and benefited from the money was to pay the pawnbrokers back, and they would restore the property. There was not a lot of interest to pay as that had been suspended throughout the investigation. They weren't happy with what I had to say and complained. In my view, they were quite outrageous in trying to use police to help their daughter succeed in a crime. I was having nothing of it. I was called in by the DI, and he told me to restore the property back to the owners. I went to my immediate supervisor, explained the problem, and asked for advice. The advice I got was unequivocal. Under no circumstances do I restore the property to the victims. The brokers had proprietary right over it. The DI did not want to put it down, but it was decided that he was not issuing a lawful order. If I was to do what he said, I would be guilty of a theft or a deception or some such thing, and the pawnbrokers would have fought it in any case. He turned out to come very close to the worst DI I had ever worked under. Fortunately, he was never my immediate

DI so I could avoid. He is a bully of the worst kind. He put intolerable pressure on his officers to rush investigations to make him look good.

Murder Most Foul?

One late turn shift (3 p.m. to 11 p.m.), I was sitting in the office, settling down to an evening of whatever London could throw at me. My other colleagues were off dealing with something or other, and my DI had just gone home for the evening. The inevitable telephone call came to break my relative peace. It was from our local control room stating that they 'thought' they had a suspicious death on their hands. The brief circumstances were that a bus had run a man over and killed him instantly. Traffic division were dispatched to deal with it as a fatal accident. They did a few basic enquiries and found that the victim had been hit over the head with a baseball bat immediately prior to falling under the bus. He didn't stand a chance and died instantly. The suspects ran off, jumped into a car, and screeched off. There was no doubt about it. Even a layman could figure that one out.

I went down to the control room and spoke to the supervisor. I could see on the CCTV that the road had been cordoned off and the scene preserved. I told them that I would call the DI and attend the scene as soon as he arrived. I called the DI. He was just walking through his front door at the time, but he turned around and came back to the office after I had related the circumstances. We went straight out to the scene on his arrival at the office. When we got there, the cordons had been removed.

There were no police officers preserving the scene. There were two people there: one uniformed traffic officer and one photographer. The traffic officer started by saying, 'I suppose we are going to have an argument about whose remit this will be.' There had been no forensic examination of the scene. The murder squad had not even been informed at this stage. Members of the public were walking all over the crime scene, and the bus, which is also considered a separate crime scene in itself, was sitting there unattended. In fact, the traffic officer wanted to jump into it and do brake tests.

In any crime scene that would need forensic examination, everything should be left in situ untouched. The scene needs to be secured so that the least amount of contamination is suffered, and people in white paper suits have to come and work their magic. All this had been abandoned. Despite the officers thinking that it was worthy of informing the CID as a potential murder, they carried on as if it was a minor fender bender. To make matters worse, the DI did nothing about it. He did not insist that the cordons go back up. I know that much of the potential evidence had been corrupted, but that didn't mean you couldn't retrieve the situation and try to preserve whatever was left. He decided that he would walk all over the crime scene in his work suit and try to find blood splatters (obviously further contaminating the crime scene).

Information, by this time, had come to us that the car had been found three miles from its registered address burned out. The DI, still not thinking it was time to reset the cordon, decided to seek advice from the HAT (Homicide Assessment Team) car. It was only when they said something to the effect of, 'What the (string of expletives) are you doing? Get those cordons in now! Extend them to take in the entire road!' Red-faced, he turned to me and asked if I could contact the control room and get the uniformed officers back to man the cordons. There was only the DI and I, and both of us were in plain clothes, so we couldn't effectively man cordons.

We then waited two hours before the uniformed officers dragged themselves back. They whinged and bleated and clearly didn't think that any of this was worth their precious time. Clearly, the victim meant nothing whatsoever to them, and they couldn't care less about the investigation. That was something that the CID could worry about. The DI, meanwhile, did and said nothing. The uniformed inspector, who had made the decision that he didn't want his officers manning the cordons, was never spoken to and asked to justify his unjustifiable decision (at least he made a decision).

My DI never chased them up while the scene was slowly being dismantled by innocent passers-by over the two-hour period we were made to wait, and when one officer told me that if someone wanted to enter the cordon, he was not going to bother to stop them. It was up to me to tell him that if he did not do as he was told, he would find himself answering questions regarding dereliction of duty. All this came about because that DI could not make a decision if his life depended on it.

He spent the next two years ensuring that any decision that could come back to bite someone in the bum would always be taken by someone else. I suppose his ethos was if you don't make any decisions, you can't make any bad ones. If you don't make bad decisions, your promotion prospects can't be harmed. He left on promotion after two years to push paper clips around some office in New Scotland Yard. They can have him!

FAMILY PLANNING

My next DI had the opposite problem. Every incident had the potential to make her career. In every situation, regardless of how minor, there could be a decision that would show off her innate detective ability and drive her up through the ranks like a hot knife through butter. The metaphorical mountains and molehills were synonymous to this DI. In one department that she headed up, I was told by the DS that they would normally take on an incident, deal with it, resolve it, and only then tell her about it so that they didn't get bogged down pointless tasks that she would set.

The one incident that jumps out at me was a rather sad case where a young girl died as a result of taking ecstasy. The investigation had two strings to it: firstly, how she died; and secondly, who supplied her with the drugs. Neither question was difficult. A post-mortem confirmed the cause of death, and plenty of people at the party, from which they had come minutes before her seizure, were very quick to point the finger at the man who was holding the party. He had clearly had a bit of a windfall and had invited all his friends to sample some of his goods. He was arrested and charged with supply of the drug. Easy, eh? No, of course it wasn't that easy. I wouldn't be writing about it if it was that straightforward.

The issue was that the victim had a heart condition that was known to her. She was fully aware that any use of illicit drugs, especially uppers like ecstasy and coke, were potentially fatal to her. As far as the family was concerned, she knew this and would never take drugs. Our information was that she was associating with known drug users on a daily basis and was more than likely using regularly. The family didn't accept this and insisted that she had been forced into taking the drugs.

The DI didn't know how to tell them that they were mistaken and effectively pandered to their every wish. It is never an easy thing dealing with the loss of a young, vibrant girl with her entire life ahead of her, and we are never going to be dismissive of them, but we also have to be realistic. She also had, in the back of her mind, the idea that if they were right, they had a murder on their hands, and they were going to solve it before the murder squad took the glory. She wouldn't listen to the intelligence, wouldn't listen to her staff, and wouldn't listen to the witnesses. She just wouldn't listen. She effectively formed her own little squad.

Detectives, who were already overworked with their day jobs, were sent out on all sorts of errands. We had to reinterview everyone. We had to send her hair off for analysis. Traces of drugs are deposited in hair and remain there forever. Cutting the hair off is the only way of getting rid of it. Of course, the analysis confirmed her regular usage. I interviewed a sister. The interview was farcical. According to her, the family never argued or never had any problems whatsoever. They smiled and laughed their way through life without a care in the world. A picture of a beautiful sunny day in an idyllic meadow with lambs gambolling in the background and butterflies fluttering about was forming in my mind. A picnic being enjoyed by the whole family, someone strumming a mandolin on a blanket, and kids flying kites nearby was the life they lead every day. It just was not reality, but the DI was on a mission. There were regular trips to see the family miles outside of London.

A year later, this very straightforward investigation was still going on. It would never find out anything that we didn't already know. Eventually, she had to accept it, but it took a long time, a lot of manpower, and a lot of expense. A tragic incident, yes, but was there any need to drag out the agony? It would have been kinder to have told them at an early stage that they needed to let go and accept their loss.

TWISTING THE KNIFE

I mentioned earlier a DI who came close to being the worst DI I had ever worked with. This one will never be worsted. I had gone into another department of the CID. We had a decent DI who recognised that we were all in that department because we wanted to be there and we were all committed. Our results showed that we were being effective. In fact, the whole Criminal Investigation Department of Croydon were hitting their targets according to the statisticians, so it must be true! A change of management at Croydon came soon after, and everything went wrong. Every department was failing within three months of the new regime, and the department in which I worked was not spared. This was a department that specialised, and we liked what we did. There were precious little chance to do what you enjoyed on a division like Croydon. Despite that, our success rate went from 42 per cent to 5 per cent almost overnight.

Now, we can't blame the management. That just wouldn't do. It must be those nasty detectives. We all came in one Monday to find that the existing DI had been told that he no longer had a job in that department. This came as a complete surprise. There was absolutely no warning whatsoever. The incoming DI was incompetent at every level imaginable. Unfortunately, she was ruthless with it and would walk over anyone without a backward glance if it enhanced her horrible life.

A week later, one of the DSs phoned up to another department to speak to a fellow DS. 'He doesn't work here anymore,' came the reply.

'Oh, where has he moved to?' asked the DS.

He was informed that the person he was looking for worked in a different department and had just taken over from another DS. And who might this other DS be? It was him. He was actually being told that he was being replaced, but no one had bothered to tell him. 'I am the DS here, and no one has replaced me!' he said. A stunned and rather embarrassed silence ensued. The DS had just found out that he had suffered the same fate as the DI. No one had approached him, and no one had the courtesy to tell him that they were going to change anyone. They just did it and did not seem to care how the people involved would take it.

The new DS was also a snake in the grass. He and the new DI were clearly working together with a brief from the station commander to make changes. Rather than being open and honest, they decided to be underhanded and dishonest. By this time, I had built up a good name in the department. I had acted up as DS on several occasions to the general acceptance of my colleagues. People were comfortable coming to me for advice and to ask me to speak on their behalf. After the two top officers were unceremoniously removed, the two of them came into the office to give us a pep talk. They asked questions and said those immortal words, 'There has been a lot of sudden changes, and you are obviously unsettled. All your jobs are safe. I intend to give you a period of calm so that you can get on with your jobs.'

During their talk, I piped up on a number of occasions to point out how we dealt with things and what policy was. I caught the DI throw me a venomous look. It was out of the blue and was as a result of nothing that I could identify. From that moment, I knew that my cards had been marked. Over the next two weeks, I kept being pulled up about the most trivial things. Once, I had worked nineteen hours in one go dealing with a detainee. I was tired and ready for bed. I bailed the detainee and left for home. I had four hours sleep and return to the station to continue with the job. We are entitled to at least eleven hours between shifts, but this does not work when you have custody matters to deal with, and we often forego this right in order to get the job done.

I returned to work to be told off because I hadn't up dated the crime report before I left for home. Everything had been properly recorded in every other respect, but the computer system that we use to record our actions was not. It was so petty that I had to wonder what the motivation for having a go at me was. I was approached by one of my colleague who looked rather worried and wanted assurances that I wasn't going to be leaving the unit. I replied by saying that I didn't think that I would have a choice.

By that Friday, I had received a garbled telephone message by the previous DI. I could not understand what he had to say and couldn't make contact again. I then got a call by another colleague about thirty minutes later. She told me that the DI and the DS were going around to detectives in other departments trying to find someone to replace me. I had heard nothing of this, although it came as no surprise. They even phoned one officer at home on long-term sick leave and told him that he was replacing me. Everyone told them to go forth and multiply except for one person, and my fate was sealed.

I came in on the following Monday fully prepared. I was called in to the office and was told that I was going to be moved off the unit. 'I know,' I replied.

'What do you mean you know?'

'I was told that you were pressing people to replace me.'

'Who told you that? I did that in the strictest confidence!'

'Yes, I am aware of that as well. If you had told me what you were up to in the first place, you would not have had to do it in any sort of confidence, and you may have received a better response,' I said.

My heckles had risen by now, and I was in serious danger of saying something inappropriate. I dismissed everything she told me and told her that I wasn't interested in what she thought. She then asked when I could leave. I said that I had a period of three weeks leave as of the next week, and it wouldn't be fair to lumber a new department with that. She said that she was thinking more in terms of hours than weeks.

In her complete and utter ignorance, she imagined that the replacement, who had only dealt with very low-level crimes, was just going to sit in my chair and automatically have a full handle on all of my investigations. She was clueless. We eventually agreed that I take the rest of the week to put everything in order and start on the Monday— when I was on leave. No one had been informed that I was coming into the new unit.

One of my jobs was at the point of charging the suspect. I went through everything with the replacement. She proved disastrous and struggled from day one. Three of my jobs were not shown as being resulted when I left, but the investigations were complete. So within two weeks, there were three 'clear-ups' accredited to my replacement and the success rate improved overnight. This showed the bosses that the DI's decision was correct. Statistics eh? Don't you just love them? That was the last time I had any dealings with both of those odious people. They were both universally disliked and have both now left the division.

OUT OF THE FIRE INTO THE FRYING PAN

I have spoken about DIs that really didn't make the grade. There are as many bad ones as there are good. This job does not encourage the act of outing those who just don't make muster, especially in the upper ranks. In fact, there are far too many instances where senior officers have cocked up royally and very publicly, only to be promoted within the year.

My next tale of woe does not involve one who cannot make a decision. Far from it, he was good at making decisions. None of them were any good to anyone other than himself. At least he did make the decisions nor did he make decisions that would enhance his promotion prospects. He was far too underhanded for that! His main vice was information about everyone and anyone. Knowledge is power. As a result, he would surround himself with sycophants.

I was in the last department that I would work at Croydon. I went in there as a DC. The person in charge was actually only acting up as a DI. He wasn't fully fledged. All of his contemporaries thought he was lazy, arrogant, and lacked knowledge. When he got the opportunity to head up a department as an acting DI, all the DS in his unit breathed a huge, collective sigh of relief. I entered as a DC, but soon enough, no DS would work with him, so he encouraged those who had passed the sergeant's exam to act up.

He drafted in one guy who was laudably incompetent and openly sycophantic. He was happy to admit that he wanted the next rank, and he would do whatever it took to schmooze senior management. He did not have the confidence of any of the DCs on the unit who could do the job better than he. He would not make a decision for all the tea in China. There was a distinct path that had been worn between his desk and the DI's office because anytime anything happened, he was off to speak to the DI. Whether it was a DC telling him to sling his hook, which happened often, or a tricky decision that he did not have the confidence to make, off he would go to the DI's office to air his woes. If I were in the DI's shoes, I would have told him to sod off and sort his own problems out. He was paid to make these decisions, he should go and make them.

Our DI, however, loved it. He was getting info in abundance. This twit was his greatest source of information. He actually encouraged it. There came a point when the last substantive DS finally had his fill and left. The DI wanted a DC to act up. He looked at a man who would fit his bill ideally. He was lazy, and he would do as he was told for an easy life. He had not taken any promotion exams and had shown no ambition to do so. I, on the other hand, had. I had more experience, I had the confidence of the troops, and I had passed the promotion exam. I approached the DI and asked why I had been overlooked. He made some bullshit excuse that he did not realise that I had the requisite qualifications. If he was being honest, he would have said that he didn't want me because I didn't tug my forelock enough.

I stood my ground too much. This may well be correct, but I only ever stood my ground when I felt he was making me do something that was either illegal, unethical, or just plain old dangerous to my own career. In the end, he was backed into a corner and had no choice now that I had pointed this out. He appointed me as acting DS alongside acting sycophant. The DI was not happy about being bested by me, so he set about testing me. There were sixteen DC/trainees/DC/PC in the office. I had ten to supervise. Sycophant had six. I had to do all the night duty shifts that came along (about twice a year) as a DC. I had to work one weekend in four as a DC, and I had to take on investigations. All the while I had to fully supervise ten DCs, all with upward of twenty investigations each every week.

In the meantime, sycophant worked no night duties at all, no weekends, and took on no investigations while supervising six DCs.

I was put under immense pressure to just mark the investigations as supervised without actually properly supervising, bearing in mind I had to supervise each investigation once a week! I was fully aware that if anything went wrong with any of the investigations that I was supervising, I would be hoofed out without so much as a by-your-leave. There was no way I was going to give in to this subliminal bullying, so I refused to shortcut anything.

I kept up to date with everything, and I supported my guys. Whenever the DI put undue pressure on them, I would go into his office and argue in their favour. Whenever sycophant threw a tantrum, which was weekly if not daily sometimes, I would dress him down and put him in his place. This would have him scooting straight into the DI's office to have a whinge. I stood my ground and refused to budge. I had results, statistics, knowledge, and the backing of my troops on my side. For all his efforts, he couldn't shift me until I made the decision to move. I didn't get promotion, but my conscience is clear.

That DI will never fall on his face nor—for the matter—his sword, which would be the honourable thing. He will retire very soon, and the Met will be rid of someone who should never have been a police officer. I even suspected that he was corrupt to a minor point, but I could never prove it. With any luck, the truth will come out, and he will be in trouble. I will only do this honestly. I won't stoop to his level. I negotiated this period. And won a lot of friends but had to move on. The Sapphire Unit otherwise known as SCD2. The department that investigates rape beckoned.

MICROMANAGEMENT

This is a subject close to my heart. As the job becomes more political, decisions that are made become more and more crucial to the promotion prospects of those seeking to walk in the rarefied air of the upper echelons. The decisions made by the practitioners (i.e., the DCs and DSs) may well be ideal for the progress of an investigation, but there are times when some of those decisions need to appear to come from higher up if it is going to enhance someone else's career.

There are also times when good decisions need to be overturned for the same reason. This has meant that micromanagement has been slowly introduced.

The more effective DIs will try to minimise the effects, as they know the system does not work from a practical point of view. Then there are those who completely espouse it, believing that as they are of a higher rank, they know better. There was even one DI who stated quite clearly that the CID would be better off if it were filled with officers fresh out of training school. They didn't argue with his decisions, they just got on with it. He didn't understand that when I argued with him, it was because he was getting it wrong. He actually accused me of not caring about the job because I was always arguing with him. In my world, it is the people who argue that are the ones with the passion. Those that don't care just shrug their shoulders and do what ever it is they are told, sometimes in the knowledge that what they are doing is either wrong or at best ineffective.

During the latter years of my career, my successes in my investigation went from strength to strength. Not just in the dreaded 'clear-up' rates. I was not only charging a lot of people, but I was also getting good successes at court. In one particular year, I seldom had a time when I had less than nine impending court cases. I ended up with twelve altogether that year. In eleven of them, the defendants were convicted, although not all for the primary offence. The only one that I failed on was a case that I didn't think should have been charged in the first place, and I made my views well known at the time.

The people involved were from all sorts of backgrounds. There was a Down's Syndrome lady, someone with serious learning difficulties, an autistic boy, a 5-year-old, a prostitute, and a police employee (not a police officer). All this was done at a time when my DI and supervisors were happy to give me the reigns and let me run with the investigations. They only got involved when they had to. The very next year, there was a change in the office, and I went on to a new team with a new DI and new DS. This team refused to allow anyone to make any decisions of any description (I think they allowed me to make a decision on what I had for lunch once, grudgingly).

Anytime a job came in, the DI and two DSs would lock themselves in a room for two hours. They would then appear having apparently solved the entire thing. They would then assign people to specific tasks and then decide who would be the investigating officer. Everything was closely scrutinised and decisions made by them. During this year, I had two people charged. One was, I thought, a shoe-in for a conviction but was acquitted at court. The other case was dropped before it even got to court. There was another investigation that I had taken on, but it was taken away from me on the day the suspects were to be charged and someone else was put in charge. The case was dropped before it got to court. I was plucked out of that team by a DI who wanted me on his team. Within six weeks, I had four people charged. I think I had five court cases that year with only one acquittal. There was no micromanagement involved.

Now, clearly there are people who need to be supervised more. Such is the way of the world. The secret of being a good supervisor in any industry is to know who are the ones that need close supervision and who can be trusted with minimal attention. Unfortunately, there are too many people who are scared to make this decision in case one of the people who are being closely watched complains that they are receiving more attention than others. Equal opportunities are quoted and everyone shrinks away. It seems that everyone should be treated the same, whether you are good at your job or not. The only thing that this policy achieves is to stifle the good work of those who can do it. Eventually, everyone becomes equal in abilities. Not by lifting the not-so-good operators but to bring the good ones down to the lower levels. How can this be good? Oh yes, I remember! It strengthens the position of the DIs and above, meaning they *have* to make the decisions as no one else can. If my personal experience is anything to go by, then that would lead to less efficiency.

Anyway, It was onwards and sideways for me, and Sapphire beckoned. There is loads of rubbish talked about rape. I will give it to you in my own perspective. Make no apologies about the language used.

RAPE, A POLICEMAN'S PERSPECTIVE

The title of this uses the word 'policeman'. There is a reason for this. I am a police officer of the male variety. Rape is a thorny old subject and views differ from culture to culture, from gender to gender, and from whatever life experiences throw at people. Women can be very judgemental of other women, and they are often more resistant to being convinced by an allegation of rape. Some women, particularly those who have been through it, will want to believe everything they hear. There are women with all sorts of views ranging between these two extremes. Some men are equally as hard to convince or can be easily persuaded, but they tend to come at it from a different angle. I am therefore writing this from a male point of view and a police officer's point of view.

This monologue refers to the victims in the female gender and the suspects in the male gender. I appreciate that there are female offenders and male victims. They are a tiny minority, and writing this in a non-gender-specific way would make the whole thing difficult to read. If I offend anyone by writing in this way, then can I suggest that this is the point at which those people should stop reading this and go find a life?

I am now a detective who works within the Sapphire unit of the Met Police. This unit deals with serious sexual assaults only and takes the investigation from cradle to grave. I therefore have experience in dealing with the victims of rape, the suspects, and all the issues surrounding it. I deal with pressure groups—volunteers who offer services to victims. I deal with genuine victims, liars, genuine suspects, and people who are falsely accused. I have been a police officer for twenty-six years and a detective for over half that time. I have been investigating rapes for many years. I know what I am doing, and I enjoy doing it because I get to remove some of the nastiest, most perverted people from society.

What is it about rape? Everyone has a different opinion about it, whether it be cultural or merely a personal opinion and whether you are a member of a pressure group or just an individual. Should there be such a thing as domestic rape? If so, is it worse, not as bad as a stranger attack, or somewhere in the middle? What should a woman do when attacked? Can it ever be a case that a woman should be partly to blame? At what point can a woman reasonably say no and expect the man to stop? Are her immediate actions after an attack indicative of the way she feels about the offence? For every question, there is a multitude of different answers, and everyone seems to think that their particular take on it is the correct one.

Police are no different, and as they are an opinionated lot anyway, their voices are as loud and unconvincing as the rest. Most criminal offences are acts that are by their very nature, an offence. Rape is different. Almost every person in the world will have sex with someone else at some point in their lives. Most will have sex many times. The act itself is a perfectly reasonable, acceptable, pleasurable bodily function. It only becomes illegal when one of the parties concerned is disagreeing to the act. I suppose taking a telly out of someone's house is perfectly legal when the owner is agreeing, but this is difficult to justify if you haven't a clue who the owner is, and you have had to batter the front door down to get at it.

A tech like me should be able to dig into my vast pool of knowledge and experience and figure out what has happened in that scenario. It is a fact of life that some men and women like having sex with different partners. It is not unheard of for a woman to roll over in the morning and say, 'Mmm, that was fantastic last night . . . err, sorry, what's your name again?' And good luck to her. It has never happened to me, so I am not speaking from experience. The only time that is likely to happen to me in the foreseeable future would be if my wife came down with some horrendous disease and died.

One also has the example of prostitution—again, nothing that I can speak about with the authority of experience—but I imagine that names and addresses are not at the forefront of their conversation. So people can have sex without knowing the other person. This does not make it rape. It is still legal (the sex, not the prostitution). All we need is the consent of both parties. When investigating anything, we have to look at two things. Both have a fancy Latin name: *actus reus* where we look at what a person actually does when committing a crime, and *mens rea* where we try to figure out the person's thought processes. In most crimes, we look at both.

The mens rea in a burglary, for example, is where someone thinks, 'Mmm, that house looks like it will have some valuables worth nicking. I think I will break in and have a butchers.' The actus reus is where he actually crashes the door down and nicks the telly. In an assault, the offender is thinking, 'I don't like that bloke.' I think I will rearrange his facial features (mens rea), then he takes a swing at his target (actus reus). In each case, the act is in itself illegal so we concentrate on that. After all, I can't read people's minds, but I can analyse actions. In rape, the act of sexual intercourse is perfectly legal unless we are talking about underage. So we have to concentrate on mens rea. It is also important that we look at it from the suspect and the victim's point of view. Was she not consenting in the first place? Did she withdraw consent later on? How did she convey that to the suspect? Was he aware that consent was not given or withdrawn?

The wording of the offence is 'penetrated the vagina/anus/mouth of person X when that person did not consent, *and* person Y did not reasonably believe person X was consenting.' We have to ensure that this aspect is properly covered. Although we will never know what each individual is thinking, we can certainly make assumptions. If the account is inconsistent, we assume there must be a lie somewhere. Why is the person lying? Can we assign the reason to the issue of consent? Is there another reason for the lie, and, therefore, do we have to dig a little deeper into this thorny issue upon which every rape investigation must hinge?

Of course twenty years ago, when we were not very good at extracting and storing DNA, we had no DNA database and would never consider trying to compare swab samples from a victim with an individual's DNA. In those days, when a person was questioned about an allegation, they would just say, 'No, not me! I have never touched her. I don't know what you are talking about.' We may have been able to extract semen from intimate samples, but we would not have been able to convincingly tell a jury that the semen came from a specific individual. Now, with all our technology, they know that there is danger in claiming that they have never had sexual contact if they have. If our scientists find semen, we can attribute it to the person making the denials, and if he has denied everything, there is no way back. They now tend to say, 'Yes, I had sex with her. She wanted it. She was the main player. It was all consensual!' Ironically, it puts them in a stronger position because it is so much more difficult to disprove a defence of consent.

Just for all you pedants out there, yes, I know that I cannot get DNA from semen itself. It is the stuff within the semen, normally the sperm, which provides a DNA profile. I was just trying to keep it simple.

PRESSURE GROUPS

The police service is notoriously weak at dealing with pressure groups because we never seem to want to defend ourselves. I think that some of the great and the good in our organisation are so suspicious that the hoi polloi of the police service (i.e. the practitioners, people like me) are out to trip them up, so they won't commit to defending us in case they are found complicit. When people with political agenda get on to the mass media and start to unjustifiably rip us to shreds, it seems to me that it could only do the service good if someone was to stand up and say, 'Actually, I have looked into the conduct of this incident, and without going into the details of the case for sub judice reasons, the actions of the officers were correct. We can give a full explanation after the case is complete.'

The deafening silence just leads people to believe that we can't justify our actions and therefore must be wrong. Bar stool politicians bang on about what they would have done in this or that situation and how it is the incompetence of police that is in question. These people have no idea about the legalities involved. Some police officers would love to be able to ride rough shod over the legal system if it meant getting the right result. Few police officers, if any, go as far as putting their beliefs into action. So we put up with the know-it-alls in the knowledge that we are correct in our actions. When all is said and done, all our actions are closely scrutinised and audit trails left by the ubiquitous computers. This is a fact that bar stool politicians and journalists alike fails to recognise or at least studiously ignore.

Rape pressure groups erroneously believe that all women should be believed when they make an allegation. In actual fact, from an investigative point of view, we should not be making decisions about believing or disbelieving anyone until we have all the facts. It is their contention that something like 95 per cent of women who make the allegations are telling the truth. They get this idea because of official statistics. As we all know, official stats very seldom reflect reality. I have no reliable statistics myself, but it is my contention that the number of allegations made broadly reflects the number of rapes that occur in the London. Unfortunately, there are a substantial number of women who simply do not report incidents of rape for any number of reasons. This is a subject that will be thoroughly explored later on, but it doesn't take a genius to work out that if these two statements are anything like correct, it must follow that not all rapes that are alleged are, in fact, true rapes. Unfortunately, within the number of allegations made, there are a substantial number of women who are being dishonest and another group who are mistaken in their belief that they have been raped. I will explain this later on, but the point is that taking figures from official statistic will not get you the full picture.

The other 'pressure group' that I have to put up with is my own senior management. Most of them are chasing around after these ridiculous statistics as if their careers depended on it. Unfortunately, it is more often than not a fact that their careers do depend on it. As the police service has come more and more under the control of politicians, the politicians are basically telling senior police officers that if they do not deliver, there are plenty of others who are happy to take their places. The politicians, of course, aren't interested in whether these people who are waiting in the wings are any good at their jobs. They just know that their brief will be to supply them with positive statistics to further their own tinpot careers.

So how do they show that they are delivering by using these statistics? They set policy to enable them to collect the stats that they want. They then parade their successes for all to see. What they are doing has nothing to do with policing and, more often than not, actually interferes with honest police work. Take the issue of burglary. If a statistician wants to show an increase in burglary so that he can swift more cash out of the government pot, he will make sure that any time a person thinks that someone tried to enter his house, it is recorded as an attempted burglary. Things like jemmy marks on doors and window are viewed as clear signs that someone has tried to break in. What other explanation can anyone ever have?

Burglary figures shoot up for a while. Money is purloined from the already-stretched coffers to finance burglary initiatives. Detectives are then told to collect the names of identified suspects, and instead of going out and arresting them—as they normally would—they put them into the operational pot. Plans are then made to go and arrest lots of burglars. They get the media on board, then on a specific day, they all go out and make the arrests.

The press have a field day in reporting the success of the operation (that is those that want to show the police in a good light). Lots of people are charged, and everyone walks away happy. The statistician now wants to show that he has been successful. Those jemmy marks on the windows and doors suddenly become classified as criminal damage. After all, how can we prove that the person who did this was intending to steal anything? Criminal damage falls into an entirely different area of the criminal law and burglary figures drop. All the people who were arrested and charged would have been arrested and charged over a more extended period of time, so in reality, nothing has changed except for the politician who can show that he is being tough on crime!

We often see fictional detectives on television. I have never understood why the heroes are always detective chief inspectors (Morse), detective inspectors (Frost), detective superintendents (*Prime Suspect*), and even a chief constable. I have only seen one detective inspector investigate anything in the last fifteen years, and that was because he was investigating a Met police sergeant. We cannot expect detectives to investigate police officers who are of senior rank to themselves. It is always at least one rank above the suspect. DCIs and above never leave the office other than to go home at the end of the day. I am not saying that they don't do anything, all I am saying is they *never* interview suspects, knock on doors, take statements, make arrests, or have anything to do with investigations in any way. It is all we can do to get them out of their offices. Even when they are involved in conferences, they use electronic gizmos, so they don't have to go out into the big, wide world and risk bumping into fellow police officers—or even worse, members of the public.

What they do have a habit of doing is making demands on the investigators if their statistics aren't looking good for them. 'Performance indicators' is the buzzword these days. It happens in all public service organisations, and the police are not exempted. We have to answer telephone calls within a certain amount of rings, we have to get to emergency calls in a certain amount of minutes, and we have to arrest a certain amount of people. In the case of some offences, we have to arrest people within a certain number of days after the offence, and we have to get a certain number of 'clear-ups'. A delightful phrase, which does not mean 'solve', it means either charged or cautioned. Your investigation is not successful unless you have charged or cautioned someone.

On the surface, this sounds fine, but what if you investigate an offence and find out that it has not happened? You have used your detective skills to discover exactly what happened, when, where, how, and with whom, but that evidence *proves* that it did not happen. In my view, I have 'solved' the case. Official figures will show it to be unsolved as there is no charge or caution. Sometimes, they will even show it is a 'no crime', which simply means that it does not get involved in any of the statistics at all. This, of course, means that when we find out that someone is lying, the investigation is no longer a rape investigation. It isn't even a criminal investigation. Officially, we have one less rape, and no one is shown to be lying about their attack. Our delightful pressure groups do not see that particular figure and their contention that 95 per cent of women are telling the truth is justified.

Another pressure group is journalists. 'Never let the truth get in the way of a good story,' we hear them say jokingly. But how much of them are saying that this statement is uncomfortably close to the truth? There are newspapers out there that seem to revel in dragging the police through the mud. The same newspapers (and I am not sure how accurate that word 'newspaper' is) will baulk at so-called good news stories about police. What do these rags have against the police? Unfortunately, there are a significant number of people who believe everything they read. There is another group who like to cherry-pick what they want to believe. It is these people who walk away thinking that the Met is just a bunch of Keystone Cops characters tripping over their own shoelaces.

Of course, the politicians start breast-beating about it, and the senior management in the police start putting in place policies to sort out the 'problems' that these rags bring to the public attention. There are plenty of real problems in the police and plenty of ways that we can improve—very few if any of these problems are brought to light by gutter press. When the police start changing the way they do things on the back of these rants, everyone—quite reasonably—then thinks that the police must have been wrong. Of course, these rags would never dream of printing retractions when it is found that they were wrong. By that time, they are already on a new subject and trying to destroy the faith that the public have in our police service in an entirely different way.

Our management either don't have the gumption or the political will to justify our actions, thereby restoring faith in police. The politicians are quite happy to see the police dragged down by the press. If anything goes horribly wrong, they blame the police and justify it by quoting newspapers. If it all turns out to be all perfectly correct, then it is they who have got it right. Of course, many newspapers are quite supportive and most are neutral, but there is nothing like sensationalism to get a story going.

HOW DO WE DO IT?

This is a quick run through what happens throughout the life of an investigation. I will add meat to the bones later on.

An investigation team comprises of a Sexual Offences Investigation Techniques (SOIT) trained officer, who is the single point of contact (SPOC) for the victim; a detective who takes on the investigation from cradle to grave; a detective sergeant who does all the supervisions and guides the investigation where there is a need; and a detective inspector who is the overall decision maker. There are also crime scene examiners variously known as scenes of crime officers (SOCO), identification officers (IDO), crime scene managers (CSM), depending on where you are based and/or which era you come from. Beyond them are all the scientists who extract DNA and do comparisons to try to identify the suspect, lab techs who do the computers and phones, Haven doctors and nurses, CPS, and an army of other people, depending on the circumstances.

In murder investigation teams, there is a definite pyramid. There are several teams, each comprising a dozen or so detectives (DC), three or four detective sergeants (DS), and a DI for each team. All the teams in each area are overlooked by DCIs, and at the top of the pile are detective superintendents and detective chief superintendents. When a murder comes in, an entire team takes on the investigation with the senior investigating officer (SIO) in overall charge. In the rape unit, the 'pyramid' is somewhat narrower. Each team comprises two or three DC, two or three SOIT, one DS, and one DI. When an allegation comes in, it is dealt with by one DC and one SOIT, with the DS having an overview. The day-to-day decisions are made by the DC and ratified up the ladder.

Don't you just love how we love an acronym in the police! There are loads: Senior Management Team (SMT); Safer Neighbourhoods Team (SNT); Murder Investigation Team (MIT); Homicide Assessment Team (HAT); Serious Crime Directorate (SCD), which has just changed to Serious Crime and Operations (SC&O); Association of Chief Police Officers (ACPO); and so on. My favourite should have been the finance and resources team, but they insisted on F&R. Killjoys! What you end up with is a MIT, part of what used to be SCD1 now called SC&O1, which comprises of DCs (some of whom get assigned to HAT), DSs, DIs, DCIs—all of whom have come up through the CID all run by ACPO as part of the MPS (Metropolitan Police Service). Alphabet soup!

When police get a call alleging rape, a uniformed response unit attends and takes an initial account. If the suspect is close by, immediate efforts are made to effect an arrest. If he is known, another unit that has had no contact with the victim, scene, or officers attending the victim should be sent to make the arrest. The scene of the crime should be identified and secured, witnesses identified, and other evidence secured. The victim has mouth swabs taken, and they are asked for a urine sample. Our unit is then called and an SOIT officer assigned. That officer will go out and speak to the victim in person. An appointment with 'the Haven' is then arranged.

The Haven is a department of the NHS that deals with examinations of victims of rape and sexual assault. They are based at four hospitals around London and work twenty-four hours a day. Once an SOIT officer calls them, they will, where possible, arrange for them to go there immediately; and if that is impossible, then they will arrange it for the very earliest opportunity. Rape relies upon obtaining physical evidence as soon as possible. It is unusual that a victim is not seen within the first few hours of the incident coming to the attention of the Haven. Because of the nature of the act, evidence can be washed away very quickly, so time is of the essence. As the investigation officer, I would liaise with the SOIT officer throughout the investigation and would make contact with the victim through them.

My job is the overall investigation. This would include the gathering of CCTV, statements from witnesses, collecting of evidence from the crime scene with the help of the SOCO, telephone examinations, computer examination, and of course dealing with the suspect.

As we all know, CCTV is ubiquitous. We are all being videoed wherever we go in public. This CCTV seldom gives us a starting point to an investigation. It rarely proves any offences and is pretty useless in the vast majority of cases. It can occasionally help identify some individuals, although this is rare, and only if the camera is zoomed in and focused on an event where the suspect happens to be. Despite this, court cases have been thrown out in the past just because CCTV has not been disclosed even if it did not show anything. CCTV, therefore, looms large in many investigations. It takes up a lot of time for very little return.

There was one occasion when the council CCTV were zoomed in on a young girl who was clearly drunk. Whether the operators were laughing at her drunkenness, ogling her skimpy attire, or observing her due to their genuine concerns for her welfare is not for me to say. The fact is that, as they were observing her, two youths approached and robbed her. Police were dispatched immediately with a perfect description, excellent footage, and a location of the victim. They were able to keep an eye on the suspects and guide the police in. Two horrible robbers bagged and property returned to victim. Unfortunately, this is the exception not the rule.

Witness statements are a little strange in these cases. After all, how often does one get an eyewitness to a rape? I am told—and I don't know how accurate it is—but in some Arabic states, you can only prove a rape if there is at least three male eyewitnesses! I hope that is an urban myth. In this country, we deal with it slightly differently. The law does not normally allow hearsay evidence in court. That is to say that one cannot give evidence of what someone else has seen or done unless they have seen it or heard it for themselves. In rape cases, they will accept hearsay in one respect. What they are looking for is exactly what the victim says to the very first person they tell.

Take for example a woman who is bashed on the head, dragged into a bush, and raped by a stranger. The stranger makes good his escape, leaving the victim semi-clad, dishevelled, and in an emotional turmoil. She gathers herself together, goes tearing out of the bush, and grabs the first person she sees. Does she calmly ask that person for a fag, chat about the weather, and mention in passing that a stranger has just raped her? Or is she sobbing and barely able to talk coherently and just pointing and sobbing?

As you can imagine, the latter scenario is very powerful evidence, especially if the person confronted is a stranger themselves. So this statement can set the scene of the immediate aftermath. It can describe the physical and emotional state of the victim and will say something like, 'I found it difficult to get out of her what had happened because she was sobbing, but I eventually got out of her that she had been raped.' Other statements taken from people she knows can go into what she had been like during the day. They can corroborate her movements. This is especially important where the victim had been out drinking and claims to have had their drink spiked.

The crime scene is always a thorny issue. Supervisors of uniformed response teams do not want to be securing crime scenes because it is manpower intensive, but if the scene is not secured, then it loses its integrity. I cannot evidence the fact that no one has been in or out of the scene unless I can turn to a police officer who has been there throughout. Some officers would want to lock the door of the premises where the crime had happened and then walk away thinking that the scene is now secure. Two problems with that: firstly, how do we know that no one else has a key, and, therefore, how can we be sure no one else has entered?

I dealt with a case once where this happened. The officer described the scene and where I would find the bedclothes. When I got to the crime scene, the door was still locked. When we entered, the washing machine was on, and the bedclothes were being washed. No one was in the premises, but someone had clearly come and gone. Evidence lost! This would not have happened if an officer had remained at the address. Even if we know that no other keys existed, what is to stop someone from simply breaking in and destroying the evidence? Secondly, what is to stop someone from breaking in to the property and removing evidence?

My personal view is that the tail is wagging the dog when it comes to crime scenes. The person in charge of the SOCOs is the borough forensic manager or the BFM (yes, more acronyms). This is etymologically incorrect. The word forensic comes from the Latin word 'forum', which was the place in Rome where senators would debate issues of the day and where people would go to complain that so-and-so stole his cow or broke his plant pot or whatever else he wanted to whinge about. The senators in the forum would hear the complaint and make decision on how to resolve it. Basically, it was an early type of law court, so the word forensic actually means for or on behalf of the law court.

Everything I do in an investigation is forensics: the taking of statements, the recording of actions, even the handing over of an exhibit from one person to another. I have heard a judge describe his words as 'forensic language'. The BFM deals with only one aspect of forensic evidence and that is forensic science. This would include fingerprints, DNA, blood splatters, points of entry, and all sorts of other work. The BFMs basic job is to balance the books. They will do this quite ruthlessly on occasions. Never mind the idea that rape is the second worst offence that can be committed behind murder. If it is going to damage their budget, you will not get the work that you require. I have actually known a BFM say to me that they would not authorise work to be carried out because they 'might not find anything'. Surely, the point is that they might find something, and that something will assist in solving the case. Your average BFM is not interested in whether you solve the case as long as their budget is fine.

Of course, BFMs have their own little performance criteria, which they will chase relentlessly whether or not the thing they are chasing is of evidential value or not. One performance indicator that they have is that if an individual is identified through fingerprints or DNA, this identification should be chased up; and in their minds, the person identified should be arrested forthwith.

Sometimes, our investigation shows that the individual is an innocent party and should therefore not be arrested. In the case of a rape, a female will make the allegation of rape by a stranger. Intimate swabs are then sent to the lab to try to identify the suspect. Sometimes, someone is identified. My next job is to speak to the victim and ask if she knows the individual and whether she has had sexual contact with that person consensually. It could, after all, be her boyfriend. If she tells us that he is not the suspect, that individual will not be arrested. He may be spoken to as a witness. The point is that the BFM will often be disappointed. I don't lose sleep over that. I am not here to enhance people's promotion prospects. I am here to solve crime.

I am the person who is responsible for the investigation or what should be described as the 'forensic strategy'. We now have SOCOs being instructed to put forward a forensic strategy. This is done without bothering to speak to the investigating officer and often deals with tasks that are so obvious it is embarrassing to read. I am the person who will be criticised if something is not done properly, especially if it causes the collapse of a case. When I want the SOCO to examine premises, do you think I can? No, they will insist on a full account from the victim and the suspect, so they can narrow their search to the smallest possible area. When this is a house or a flat, the danger is always going to be that they miss something. Never mind that one or both will lie to us, what if they simply forget something? If the SOCO works on that information and only then a day later more information comes to light, it is now too late as the scene is no longer secured.

As I have mentioned earlier, we can't believe or disbelieve anyone at this early part of the investigation, so we have to gather as much information as we can. Surely, as the investigating officer responsible for the entirety of the investigation strategy, the BFM should be taking our views into account much more. Unfortunately, they are only interested in one thing: how can we get through this investigation by spending as little money as we can? Sod the victim or, for that matter, the suspect; my budget is more important. I agree that we, as a public service, have to be aware of not squandering money. We also have a duty to victims of crime and to the future potential victims of the suspect.

Once inside the scene, generally speaking, I am consulted very closely and most of what I require is done. But even then, they will quite often scoop up all sorts of interesting things that I, as an investigator, will never be able to use. These items then just clog up the property store.

Dealing with the suspect takes on all sorts of different aspects, depending on all sorts of variables. This will be gone into more thoroughly. We talk about crime scenes a lot. Most people think of a cordoned off area, sometimes even a tented area, where IDOs are wandering in and out dressed in their sexy crime scene overalls, booties, and hair covers. What we don't consider is that the victim is a 'crime scene' and the suspect is also a 'crime scene', so when a suspect is arrested soon after an offence has been committed, he has to be examined as such. This includes intimate swabs as well as hand swabs, and when we have finished thoroughly humiliating the suspect, then we interview.

Once all the evidence is gathered, we have the opportunity to put the case to the Crown Prosecution Service (CPS). Now here's a thing. During the last government, a lot was made of league tables and performance criteria. This is not just because the last government wanted to have figures to justify their own position, although that is a big part of it. The other reason is that computers have taken over the world. This means that statistics can be extrapolated much more easily than in the past. One can also massage figures and make them say what you want them to say. This must be hours of fun for your averagely ambitious politician.

In the case of police, as previously stated, there were all sorts of performance indicators—none of which were good indications of how individuals performed, but it kept the politicians happy. The main performance indicator is the 'clear-up'. This is just another name for 'solve'. Because it is all computer-based, the way they get their stats is to look to see how many people are charged or cautioned. The more they get, the better they are doing. This is rubbish of the highest order.

When I investigate a crime, I am trying to work out what happened. If I find out what happened, I believe I have 'solved' it. If what I discover is that the offence did not happen, then there is no way I can charge anyone. Despite this, the investigation will be recorded as unsolved, as I have not been able to charge someone.

This is neither here nor there as far as the CPS are concerned. The police have to charge as many people as possible to show that they are working properly. The powers-that-be in the police are not interested in what happens at court. That is the lot of the CPS. The CPS have to get convictions to show that they are working properly. When all these ideas about performance indicators were floating around, the government decided to give the CPS the decision on whether or not to charge someone. Once upon a time, police used to make all these decisions. The CPS were there to offer advice and give their opinions, but the decision lay within the police.

It is probably true to say that we were too quick to charge sometimes. If there was some doubt then, the ethos was that we should not decide whether someone is guilty or not. That is the job of juries. It's one of those cases where we were damned if we did and damned if we didn't. If we made the decision not to charge, then we were being judge and jury and that was not fair. If we did charge on flimsy evidence, then we were wasting public funds. In the end, the Home Office took the decision away.

Now, we have a CPS who has to show that the percentage of people charged to those convicted is at/or above a certain percentage. They would also want to see a year-on-year improvement. How do they do this? Of course, the way they get a higher percentage of convictions is to never take a chance. They will want to charge only when there is overwhelming evidence. Something that is hard to come by in rape cases. They only want to charge where the proverbial fingers have been caught in the cookie jar. But they don't want a 100 per cent success rate because you can't improve on that, so they will second-guess what a jury might think and make a decision not to charge in many cases. In most cases, this is fine; but in the borderline cases, what we have is an unelected group of people making decision that a jury should be making.

From the police point of view, we have to have a pretty watertight case before they will even look at it. In rape cases, because they are so hard to prove, they want this and more. When a 14-year-old oik nicks a telephone from another 14-year-old oik, it is expected that a full investigation will take place within a day, and every effort should be made to remand the 'robber' in custody, pending a trial. When a woman is raped, the CPS will do all they can to avoid remanding in custody. I have actually seen one case where the CPS lawyer justified not making an early charging decision as the suspect 'did not pose a danger'. I wonder what most rape victims would feel if they knew that their attacker was deemed as not posing a danger in their cases. If a rapist is not a danger to society, who the hell is?

We get past the CPS and manage to charge our suspect and then the work starts. Prepping for court can be very fraught. Time limits set by the court come in where paperwork has to be served in a certain time. Case management hearings to check that the case is progressing properly are a regular feature. Judge's orders must be adhered to. Although the police management no longer care about what is happening to the case because they have their clear-up, my job begins in earnest. (Yes, that does appear to mean that my management don't care about half of what I do. Great, isn't it?)

One part of English law is our requirement to disclose our case to the defence. Fair enough, but if the defence want any more than the basics, we get into a quid pro quo scenario: if you want us to disclose material that will assist your defence, we need to know what your defence is. So if you give us your defence statement, we will give you anything you ask for—as long as it assists your defence. What this means to us is that we get a brief preview of what they are intending to say. This can be a double-edged sword.

We then get to trial where my interviews with the victim and suspect are hacked to pieces by clever defence people. The jury are left in the dark about half of the evidence. Legal arguments about what the jury can and cannot hear are heard.

Here is where a lot of misconceptions about rape come to the fore. In my experience of juries—and I have been a juror twice myself—they either do not understand or are not interested in whether they are sure that the prosecution have proved the case. There are plenty of people out there who come from different countries where they do not believe there is such a thing as domestic rape. They will then just go with their belief and the law of their own land and acquit regardless of evidence.

Different countries have different ideas on when a person is mature enough to give consent to sex. Some are as young as twelve; some believe that when a woman starts menstruating, they are fit to marry. Again, they will take their beliefs into court and acquit. Women on juries tend to judge female victims harshly and ignore evidence, and there are men out there from all backgrounds who just believe that a woman can stop an attack if they really wanted to in any circumstances. Unfortunately, all these people find themselves on juries, and dangerous men are allowed back out on the street as a result. Let us take each element of the investigation in order.

Initial Response

There are 30,000 police in the Met. Not all of us think the same, not all of us have the same work ethos, and not all of us have the same experience of life or of working as a police officer. We have a large number of officers from different cultural and ethnic backgrounds. The ratio of male to female has improved hugely in the past twenty-five years. What this means is that there are 30,000 different ways that officers deal with allegations. Because rape is such an emotive subject, these differences are magnified.

It is here that I will have to deal with another elephant in the room. Some people who make allegations of rape are lying. The allegations can be malicious, and there are many reasons why this might be. I am aware that the breast-beaters and pressure groups will read that statement as 'police believe all women lie about rape'. Nothing could be further from the truth.

When someone calls the police, it is invariably a uniform response office who will take the initial allegation. A uniformed officer will quickly make their minds up as to whether they think the allegation has any foundation at all. Most of the time, this is reasonably accurate. The problem is that a small but significant number are wrong. When I say this, I mean sometimes they think the allegation is a pack of lies, and investigation discovers that it is in fact true. Equally, some officers make the decision that the person making the allegation is truthful and investigation reveals a web of lies. All this appears to be fine because the investigation is what counts. Unfortunately, the view of the initial reporting officer often dictates how he/she deals with the victim.

As we all know from watching *CSI: Outer Hebrides* or whatever it is (never watched any of them). The first hour in any investigation is crucial and can make or break an investigation. We like to call it the golden hour. I think there is also a platinum fifteen minutes, or something similar, but I suspect this was just some senior officer trying to invent something to improve his/her chances of the next promotion. The long and the short of it is that if the first officer on scene is convinced that a woman has been raped. All the stops will be pulled. Everything that should be done is done and more. Swabs are taken, clothing seized and properly sealed and recorded, suspect found and arrested, witnesses identified, and statements taken in some cases.

When it comes to my desk, I have an excellent package of everything that has been done. If the officer does not believe the victim, everything is lacklustre. If they trip over the suspect, they will arrest. No witnesses identified, no swabs, no evidential property seized. When it gets to my desk two or three hours after the first call is made, I have nothing other than a distraught victim who thinks all police are idiots, a suspect in custody not knowing what is happening, and a 'golden hour' that is lost. This happens quite al lot. As I intimated, quite often the officer is correct. But sometimes, he is wrong, and a lot of ground is lost. This quite often means that we lose cases that could otherwise have been successful.

There was one example of this where everyone thought the woman was spinning a web of lies, and nothing she said made an iota of sense. Even the investigating officer had the same view. Fortunately, we have protocols in place and we carry on with investigations regardless of what we think. On that occasion, the initial scene was examined, and everything was done properly if not enthusiastically. The suspect was interviewed and denied any and all contact. He was released on bail, as is normally the case. She was interviewed and statements from other witnesses were taken. The victim's swabs were sent off to the lab for examination, and lo and behold, the DNA of the suspect was found in the swabs. This not only showed the suspect as lying through his back teeth but also corroborated what the victim said. He was prosecuted and found guilty. It goes to show that if we follow protocol, we have a chance.

Whenever the word 'rape' is heard, the majority of officers want to run a mile in the opposite direction. This is odd, as police officers often run *towards* danger in most other cases. But rape is put in the too-difficult box. Too difficult to deal with emotional women, too difficult to ask what are often very personal and intimate details, just plain old too difficult. In fact, it is not difficult. It is just an allegation like any other. The only difference is that you can't see any visible difference in the 'before and after'. Aside from other forms of physical violence, a woman looks just the same before a rape as she does after. When we go to report the burglary of a TV, we can see that there was a TV, and now there isn't. When someone is murdered, the before and after is relatively easy to spot.

People tend to judge women in many cases. I am not just talking about police. It tends to run right the way through society. I have a world exclusive: prostitutes can be raped! Women who like to have sex with different partners can be raped. We all like to think we live in enlightened times, but we still think of women who like sex as having 'loose morals' whereas men are just playing the field. I am not just talking about what men think. I have heard plenty of women talking about sexually very active women in less than complimentary terms. We need to cut through all this rubbish and try to find the facts. It is true that it makes it more difficult when the lab report comes back showing five different male contributors within the intimate swabs of a victim, but is that not what investigation is about? Sorting the wheat from the chaff, figuring whodunnit, and gathering the evidence to show what happened? As long as the victim is being truthful from the off, the reporting officer should treat it as any other allegation.

A few years ago, people with learning difficulties or other mental problems would never get a look in. They would be brushed aside, as officers and the CPS would claim that we just couldn't get through the mental difficulties. The victim will be made to look a liar in court by clever defences. The suspect is more believable, the victim can't be relied upon, and so on. Initial investigating officers are improving in this field. Many are realising that women with mental difficulties are actually targeted, as the suspects think that no one will believe them. It is gratifying to see this change and even more gratifying to see the predators getting convicted. We use all sorts of experts to cut through the fog now, so an initial allegation, although it may be difficult, is not impossible; and as long as all the initial bits are done properly, we always stand a fighting chance.

The response officers have a minefield to wade through in pretty much everything they do. If preconceptions are left at home and each job is properly dealt with, we do get the results. I know that most officers want to do the best for genuine victims. It is how we find out who the genuine victims are, and how we deal with the victims and those that stand accused that should define our investigations.

SOIT

Predominantly, women—although there are some men who take this role—are the people who effectively gather the information from the victims of rape. It is this information that I require in order to start an investigation. They have a specific way of dealing with victims. They are, first and foremost, police officers who are investigating a serious event. They are evidence gatherers. They get to know the victim and try to make them feel as comfortable as possible. This is difficult enough. Let's face it. How comfortable would anyone be when talking to a complete stranger about their sexual activity? I suppose sometimes, it may be easier to speak to a faceless police officer in the same way that you would talk to a brick wall, but generally, this subject is not something that people easily talk about.

An SOIT officer will never challenge an account initially unless it is so ludicrous that they absolutely have to. So the first question is 'what happened?' Some women say virtually nothing. Others just blurt everything out almost as a release. The SOIT will then go about collecting sufficient information to initiate the investigation by asking questions and developing the account given. This necessarily has to deal with specifics: what part of him went into which part of you? Without that information, the investigation falters before it starts.

Then it is off to the Haven. As long as she is sober, lucid, and able to consent to an intimate examination, the Haven doctor and nurse will receive her at their next available appointment. If the victim is not sober, the doctors say that they won't be able to give their considered consent for the examination. If they were to go ahead regardless, they could be accused of sexual assault. So drunk people have to sober up even if it means evidence lost. If lucky, they will get an appointment straight away. Sometimes, there is a wait for several hours. This can be uncomfortable because police will be asking the victim to avoid washing or urinating where possible. The doctors at the Haven perform forensic examinations, both internal and external. They record injuries, take intimate samples, and offer advice about STDs and the morning after pill where appropriate.

The examinations are normally thorough and go on for two to three hours. The doctors will then hand all the swabs and any other evidence like clothing, etc. to police for use in the investigation. Despite the fact that it is a 'forensic exam', they won't release anything other than basic information unless the victim signs a disclaimer. This, then, can be used in evidence.

Now comes the statement. This is the job of the SOIT, and it is their bread and butter. They receive extensive training on best practise. They normally do a video-recorded statement. The reason for this is so that the victim does not have to then keep reliving her experience. The video can be played in court instead of her going through everything again and again. This will not negate the requirement for her to attend court, as the defence will want to cross-examine her.

So how do we deal with this statement? We ask questions—lots of them. The powers that be have made a decision that all victims of rape are to be believed. This is *not* what happens in reality. As a detective, I have to take any and all information and dispassionately investigate the facts when starting out an investigation. I have to go where the evidence leads me. If that is away from what the victim tells me, then so be it. It is not a case of believing or disbelieving anyone initially. Once the facts are all collated, and the evidence proves that the offence has been committed, then and only then do we 'believe' the victim.

We then set out to prove the allegation to a forensic standard. It is at this point when we are no longer impartial because we become part of the prosecution team. Before this point, we have to remain impartial and are often accused of being otherwise by the defence counsel in the case of suspects charged or victims in the case of investigations being dropped prior to charge.

Having said all that, it is not good to start challenging the victim of a rape from the outset unless there are obvious problems with the initial account. Officers should then go into the victim and ask as many questions as possible to develop the account. She will normally give a very brief idea of what has happened. This is quite natural. They are talking to a perfect stranger about some very intimate details. Tact is necessary in bucket loads. Underlying all those questions is the idea that if she is telling the truth, it does not matter what questions you put, how you put them, and what direction you are coming from. The answers are going to be the same, and they are going to be consistent. If it is all a lie, then we will find out.

The theory is that memories are created by events. The more information one has about the event, the stronger the memory. If you pass a stranger in the street and nothing is said or done, it is unlikely you will remember. If that stranger stamps on your foot and swears at you for no apparent reason, that memory will stick with you for some time to come. In the same way, an event like a rape is going to stick for all sorts of reasons . . . if it happened. If it did not happen and you are lying, then the 'event' you are remembering is the actual lie you have told. You are taking information from your imagination and not your memory. The more questions we ask, the more you have to remember what you have said; and as your memory has not been stimulated by the physical act, you will struggle.

At this point, the SOIT is still not challenging anything they say. The account is developed in fine detail, the questions are put, and the finest detail is extracted from the victim. This needs to be done for several reasons. I have previously gone into the use of lots of questions in order to test the veracity of the account. We will also need the information to decide what we need to get from the labs. We use her account to test the evidence with the suspect. Mainly, we need this information because the legal system in this country will allow the defence to cast doubt on anything that may have a double meaning or may be a little unclear. The defence will naturally try to clarify it in their own way. This will obviously be in order to paint their client as the innocent party. The SOIT will therefore ask very specific questions.

Thereafter, it is just a case of maintaining contact, letting them know how the investigation is progressing, letting them know if there is a decision to take no further action, or to charge. If it is a charge, it is a case of preparing her for the court case.

Rape is not about sex; it is about violence, control, and humiliation. A rapist will seldom plead guilty at court, especially in domestic situations, because the attacker's only hold they have on the victim once he is charged is the fact that they can make them relive everything in front of a load of strangers in the form of a jury. He can also instruct his defence to put a series of questions to her that will humiliate her. The court proceedings are therefore just an extension of the original rape—a way of maintaining some kind of control and a way of humiliating her. We, as police, try to mitigate this hold they have on the victim. Video statements are one such method. We use screens in court so that the victim need not be intimidated by having to look her attacker in the face while he grins at her. The SOIT officer will explain all of this during the course of the investigation.

Many victims are very needy and constantly call the SOIT officers. Some just wait for contact, some even break contact completely. The SOIT officer is there to keep them on board. It is a very stressful time for most, and extreme tact needs to be used while maintaining honesty. This essentially means that the victim should be left in no doubt that they aren't going to be treated with kid gloves in court. It also means that if there is little chance of getting a charge, they should be aware of this so that they are not so devastated when that decision comes.

The relationship between the SOIT and the officer is important because there has to be trust that the detective will follow all the leads, and the SOIT will extract the information required. The detective is normally directly involved in the video interview anyway. They are normally operating the video equipment from a different room and will be listening to the interview. He will have his opportunity to ask the interviewer to put questions that he thinks pertinent. It is sometimes at this point that a challenge might go in. This is normally avoided until much later, but if it means that the investigation goes in the right direction, then so be it.

It is a little known fact that detectives get charges, and SOIT officers get convictions. It is they who extract the information that is required, and the better the interviewer, the more information we have, the better the chance of success.

VICTIM

———— • ————

Where do I start? I could write a book about this part of this subject. Some women, in particular those who have suffered domestic violence, don't like to be called victims. They prefer the word 'survivors' because of the message that the word 'victim' evokes. I am a 50-year-old crusty, old fart who believes in simple language. 'What's in a name? That which we call a rose by any other name would smell as sweet.' I will continue to use the word victim for the purposes of this.

The 'victim' is where any investigation has to start and end. No one can anticipate what people are going to say next. Every individual will act differently, and each reaction is neither right nor wrong. Those who have never been in the position of the victim will often criticise them for not doing this or for doing that. I have heard it all, and for all the efforts I put in to try to defend genuine victims, my words are ignored. I will just say that one should never judge until one has been in their position.

I suppose the classic example is the fight or flight response. Some people fight, some people flea. It doesn't matter who you are, how strong you are, or whether or not you have a propensity to violence. You will not know how you react until it happens. Rape is the same. If a man approaches and says 'do as I say and you won't get hurt', do you protest? Some will and some won't. Can we criticise that person who didn't protest? I don't think we can. Would a woman be prepared to bear extensive facial scarring for the rest of her life and avoid being raped, or would she put up with the prospect of mental scarring and save her face? This is not a choice I would want to have to make.

I have had CPS make decisions to drop cases because they couldn't understand why the victim didn't call out. It is very difficult to explain why you don't shout out or try to get someone's attention, but I don't think we should judge others for it. This is a very traumatic time. They are being humiliated. They are being overpowered. Who is going to shout out and say, 'Look, what this man is doing to me, he is doing this awful thing. Come and help me.' The question would then be: if you were so afraid and so overpowered, how could you have the time to attract all that attention?

Surely, the rapist's first concern is not getting caught. Why would he allow you to do that? I remember as a youngster talking about this subject. Someone gave the example of a judge holding up a needle and asking someone else to thread it while he held the needle. Every time the person tried to thread it, he moved it away. This, he felt, amply demonstrated the fact that if a woman didn't want to be raped, she could get away just by moving to one side. I am taking it that no one had the bottle to hold a knife to the throat of the judge, warning him that if he moved while the needle was being threaded, he would die. That may have amply demonstrated that the judge was an idiot. This was all a lifetime ago in a different world. If the judge isn't dead by now, he won't be far off, and he won't be sitting in judgement of victims anymore.

Something that often comes up is the question of why a particular woman does not call police straightaway? Why did she leave it to someone else to call the police? Why did she sit on the information for a day before calling police? I don't have statistics to hand. Mainly because I think statistics are the most unhelpful of things. It does seem to me, though, that in the majority of cases, it is someone other than the victim that calls the police. Take for example the woman who is walking down an alleyway, whistling a happy tune, and minding her own business when someone jumps out of a bush, holds a knife to her, and drags her into the bush and rapes her. A scenario that is very rare, I am happy to say. Imagine the scene. The male does his thing, pulls his trousers up, and runs off. She is left dazed and confused as she emerges from the bush semi-clad and in an emotional mess and grabs the first passer-by. The victim is in no state to start making telephone calls; it is invariably the passer-by that does that.

On the other hand, take the instance of a woman who is raped by her husband. She phones Mum in a flood of tears. Mum comes around, takes daughter out of immediate danger, and calls police or at least persuades the victim to call the police. If anything, I find that when I am dealing with any allegation, the fact that someone else has called the police adds credence in many cases. I also find that the amount of time that elapses between rape and reporting often does not detract from the veracity of the allegation. Sometimes, it can strengthen the account.

It is not unusual to find women calling the police about a domestic assault whereby she has been hit by her husband. Sometimes, it can be a neighbour who calls to report a violent domestic because the victims of domestic assault won't call police themselves. In domestic assault cases, there are protocols that police must follow. One of these is the asking of certain questions to assess the risk that is posed to the woman by her husband. One of the questions asked is whether she has been sexually assaulted by her husband. The woman will often not have considered the fact that she has been sexually abused for years. It is only at this point that we find out. We also have enough cases where a woman tells us that she has been sexually assaulted by her husband just to get her own back. No one knows how many of the rape allegations in these circumstances are true and how many are false because the official attitude is to believe them anyway. This makes the statistics even more wildly inaccurate than normal.

As to why a woman would not report straightaway, where do I start? I had a recent case where a woman with mental difficulties didn't come out of her flat for three days and didn't talk to anyone about anything. She went into herself for that three days. When she emerged, her friend realised that something was wrong and managed to get it out of her. Can we stand in judgement of her actions? I think not!

Then you have the cases where a woman is sexually abused by a family member or a friend of the family. She doesn't report it for fifteen years! Why not? Well, the answers to that are many and varied: 'I tried to tell my mother, but she told me that I was imagining things'; 'I couldn't tell anyone because I was embarrassed, and I was too young to understand what was happening.' We even have cases where the mother is complicit in the attacks. Who would a very young girl turn to then?

Of course, domestic rapes are an entirely different set of concerns as far as the victim is concerned. You always want to shout at the victims of domestic abuse and say, 'Leave the idiot, get away from him! There are plenty of men who do not feel the need to beat up women!' Unfortunately, you know that many women seem to go from one abusive relationship to the next so it makes no difference any way.

Domestic violence is about violence, control, and humiliation. Now, where have I seen that before? Oh yes, I remember. 'Rape is not about sex.' If you think about it, it is inconceivable that a man who wants to have absolute control over his wife, who is violent to his wife, and who keeps her in a constant state of humiliation and subjugation would not extend this to their sexual contact. Therefore, if a woman is in that situation, it is probable that she is being raped on a regular basis. Unfortunately, we will never know in most cases because they just won't say. Why? Because they don't want to criminalise the father of their children; because the father is their only means of support; because she still loves him, and he is a wonderful person when he is sober. There are plenty of other reasons.

Then, of course, you have the difficulty of getting around a jury. Domestic cases are not well liked by juries. I will explain this in a chapter set aside for this subject.

When dealing with the victim, we have to deal with all the aspects. As I mentioned in my opening sentences, not all women tell the truth about rape and some are simply mistaken. I will deal with the one that no one seems to want to deal with: the liar.

Whether we like it or not, there are liars out there, and we have to deal with them. If rape is the worst thing that can happen to a woman outside murder or serious maiming, then the worst thing that can happen to a man is that a woman deliberately lies about him by accusing him of rape just to get herself out of a fix. I had a case where a woman had the hots for a man who just did not see her as a sexual partner. She decided, one day, to do something that would cause him to swoop to her rescue. She met another local man, and over the next day or so, started to text him and arranged to meet up with him. They met up and had sex in the back of his van. We tracked all this just by reading the text messages that were going between the two of them. These text messages were coming in thick and fast, leading up to their meeting. One every couple of minutes of so, there was a thirty-minute cessation of texts, then a message from her telling the man that what they had just done was great and that they should get together again. Fifteen minutes later, she sent another text saying that she was not all that happy about the sex, she didn't want it, and as far as she was concerned, she had been raped. Of course, the man became a bit confused and panicky but couldn't get to the bottom of what happened.

In the meantime, she went back to her would-be lover and told him that she had been raped and pointed out who had done it and where he was. This was only two or three minutes down the road. Her friend, being a gentleman, swooped to her rescue as predicted. He jumped up and walked out the house to confront his friend's rapist. Unfortunately for the female, a police car just happened past as he got out of his house. He, being an honest citizen, decided that the police were better placed to deal with it. He flagged them down and told them what he knew. The woman was now stuck between a rock and a hard place. She couldn't tell the truth; that would destroy everything, so she had to run with it. She made her statement. She was confronted with all the texts and simply blanked them. Her statement was inconsistent and nothing added up. It was a mess.

Naturally, the case was dropped at a very early stage but not before the man had been arrested. I wanted to deal with her for perverting the course of justice or perjury or anything to send her the message that she had done something very wrong. I was not allowed. The CPS would not touch it.

I have numerous examples, and they would just start getting boring very quickly, but I have seen plenty of examples of women being caught in flagrante delicto by boyfriend/husband/girlfriend and shouted rape so that she wouldn't get into trouble with the aforementioned.

There is the other problem of domestic assaults. It is policy that whenever a woman alleges a domestic assault, they are asked a series of questions. One of these questions is essentially asking whether they suffer sexual abuse at the hands of their partner. Notwithstanding my previous comments on domestic situations, there is a danger that some women will say, 'Sod it, he hit me before and got away with it. Let's up the ante a little. That will teach him.' Then when the question comes, the answer is, 'Yes, he raped me five days ago.' This is almost impossible to prove, but the wheels are now set in motion, and we have to try to get to the bottom of it. Don't get me wrong. Any man who thinks it is good to hit someone who relies on them for their livelihood is no one who I lose any sleepover. I do, however, like to get to the truth of any incident, and in those cases, the truth is virtually impossible to find.

Because we are all sexual creatures, we also feed off our own experiences. Sometimes, we have sat in the office talking about an allegation and tried to imagine the positions they find themselves in. Some of them would have required a contortionist. The woman wedged between two men in the backseat of a tiny car, all sitting in their seats, while she is forced to give one of them a blow job. Think about it. Find a Fiat 500 and try it. Don't do it if you have a bad back!

We then have the guy who is holding a knife to the woman while forcing her legs apart with his other hand and covering her mouth to stop her screaming. He is doing this while removing her knickers and jeans forcefully and dropping his own trousers. Men don't multitask!

Let us now deal with those women who are mistaken. This will seem a little weird. Any woman will know when they have been raped, surely. Sometimes, it isn't the case. One of the most obvious mistakes is the fact that many people do not know that penetrating the mouth with a penis is also rape, so they would never report it because they simply don't know.

On the other hand, you get the cases where a woman complains to her friend or mother or counsellor or whoever she speaks to and says that hubby came home the previous night drunk as a lord, as usual, demanding sex. He is sometimes violent when he is drunk, so she says, 'Okay, get on with it. Wake me up when you are finished.' She then lays down and thinks of England, but she really didn't want to do it. Her confidante then informs her that if he had sex with her and she didn't want it, that is rape, and the police should be informed. While I agree that what happened is not pleasant, I will have to refer you back to some of my opening comments. I gave the wording of the offence of rape. The last line being '. . . and person you did not reasonably believe person X was consenting'. It cannot be considered rape if the man is not aware that consent is not given or has been withdrawn. In this scenario, she has agreed. Even if she is not exactly enthusiastic, she still allows him. Consent given, no offence committed—harsh but true.

We also have the unfortunates in society: people with mental difficulties. The lady who lived in the top floor of a block of flat and believed a man from the floor below had raped her while he was still in his room and she was in hers. Now, that has got to be a great party trick.

Some women will lie about things that they believe have little or no bearing on the case. There are a number of reasons for this. They may be trying to protect someone else, or it could be that they think that if a piece of information came out, it would show them in a bad light. This is all very well and, in some cases, quite laudable. The problem is that if I were to discover the lie, I have to disclose this to all interested parties if a person is charged. If I found something out, what is to stop anyone else finding out the same information? If I were to suppress it, the whole investigation can be brought into question. Why was the information not disclosed? How impartial was the investigation? Who would gain out of suppressing the information?

This applies regardless of the information. The defence will say that it all goes to the veracity of the allegation. I investigated a rape involving an estranged husband who had a long history of extreme violence. He actually walked around wearing stab and bulletproof vests. The investigation involved two police forces, a firearms operation, and remanding the suspect in custody while he awaited trial. It later came to our notice that her grown-up sons had got involved on the day. They had come around to the house armed to the teeth and chased the suspect off. This was never brought to our attention because the victim was aware that her sons had acted highly illegally in protecting her. She naturally wanted to protect them and so just omitted them from the account. We found out and disclosed it to the CPS. The CPS dropped the case. One very dangerous individual was released to do his nefarious deeds once more. I have never doubted that this man violently attacked her, but the CPS did not want a situation where the victim was rightly accused of lying by omission.

It is not unusual for victims to deny using illegal substances. If the suspect suggests this is the case, I have no choice but to submit urine samples for toxicology. This then becomes disclosable, and we have to do a lot of backtracking. The honesty of the victim is brought into question, and everyone seems to forget that none of this excuses the sort of violence that is being investigated. The defence team is not interested in whether or not their client is guilty. In fact, they will run a mile in order that they do not know whether they are or not. All they are interested in is whether or not they can convince the jury that the victim is lying. They will do this by dragging up anything that can show any dishonesty in their past. They then blow it up out of all proportion and hope that the jury forget about what the trial is about and start sitting in judgement on the victim instead.

Honesty is always the best policy. If it makes the victim look bad, so be it! Better the devil we know. At least we can deal with it instead of being confronted with it when it is too late.

Fortunately, most do tell the truth, and it becomes obvious after a very short while. I have mentioned that every one react differently. We are aware of that, but we still say to ourselves, 'Yes, I can see why you did that in that situation. It may not be what many people will do, but let's work with it.'

Another subject that gets people into a frazzle: at what point can a woman say no and reasonably expect a man to desist? Most of the time, it is obvious, but the black and white fades into grey at one point. It depends on who you are and what your belief structure is. Let's go through it.

1. Girl meets boy. Boy pops the question: fancy a shag? (Foreplay in today's world)
    Girl says no: game over, look for someone else.
    Girl says yes: game on!

2. Girl and boy go to his/her house, hotel room, lover's lane, or behind the bicycle shed. Both have a fondle.
    Girl says no: game over, go find someone else.
    Girl says, 'Come on, big boy!': game on.

3. Clothing starts coming off. Heavy petting ensues.
    Girl changes her mind and says no: game over, go find someone else.
    Girl starts to moan with pleasure and encourages boy: game on.

4A. Condom goes on, boy fully erect and ready for entry.
    Girl changes her mind and says no: game over, go find someone else.
    Girl presents herself and guides him towards his pleasure: game on.

4B. Neither of them have contraception.
    Girl says no: game over go find someone else.
    Girl is happy to carry on: game on.

5. Entry is complete and sex is taking place.
    Girl says she wants him to stop: game over, frustration!
    Girl is joining in and clearly enjoying the experience: game on.

6. Boy starts to reach climax.
    Girl does not want to risk pregnancy. Tries to push him off, so he ejaculates elsewhere.

The law states that a woman can say no at any time during this process. There will be very few people who will have a problem with scenario one other than the idea that some women would expect a little more effort from the boy before he gets to that stage. This is wooing in the modern day, I'm afraid. Slightly more people will have a problem with scenario two, and this proportion increases point by point. I, as an investigator, have to prove that she either did not consent in the first place or withdrew her consent. How many people will believe that she is being reasonable in taking him to the back of the bicycle sheds, removing clothing, then saying thanks but no thanks? The law is not interested in fairness, only whether she withdrew consent.

In some ways, scenario five is better for the bloke than the bicycle shed scenario. At least there may be a reason for the withdrawal. It may be hurting or someone is coming (unfortunately, not the boy in question). At least the bloke has had some satisfaction, and she is not just being a tease. Scenario six is probably the most contentious. I think Billy Connelly once said in one of his stand-up sessions that the wild horses couldn't drag him in the other direction at the point of ejaculation. He was talking about the rhythm method of contraception, but you get my drift.

SUSPECT

Everything, so far, has been in some sort of order. From here on, it very much depends on what information you have and whether or not you know who the suspect is.

The suspect is normally scooped up as quickly as possible. As previously stated, this is not always ideal, but it is what normally happens. He is, after all, a crime scene and needs to be treated as such like any other crime scene—to a point. I'm not suggesting that we would force him open, seize all his insides, and spread silver fingerprint powder all over him like we may do in a house, but you get my meaning.

He is booked in, and a sample of DNA taken. This should be done in every case where sexual offences are alleged, although it is often forgotten by some officers. If a suspect has been arrested before, we will normally have his DNA on a database. For most offences, further DNA is not required. Police do have the power to take DNA wherever a person is arrested. When the arrest is for a sexual offence, this should be done. The reason is partly from a continuity point of view. It is strong evidence if I can say, 'I took DNA from this person. That sample was used to compare with the victim's swabs.' How do I know that the person standing in front of me is definitely the person who provided the DNA that is already contained on the database? Mistakes can be made and have been made in the past! I do, however, know that he did contribute to this one.

The other reason is a little more abstract and everything to do with money. If I send off samples from a victim and DNA from someone other than her is extracted, they can compare it directly to the sample taken from the suspect that they have in their possession. If they don't have that sample, then they have to request a search of the database to see if the sample has a match. His has a cost implication. For that reason, I am not allowed to send a lab submission off without the suspect sample unless, of course, I don't know who the suspect is. They then have to swallow the cost.

Now comes the interview. Let us be perfectly clear here. There are three basic ways for a suspect to deal with an interview: no comment, tell the truth, or lie. There are obviously variations, but those are your basic choices. There are also three basic scenarios as far as the involvement of the suspect:

1. I wasn't there, I don't know what you are talking about. I was on the planet Mars at the time, playing with a remote control car.
2. I was there, but it I didn't do it. It was someone else.
3. I was there, and I did it.

Again, there are infinite number of variations to this, but this is your basic three. It has always been my contention that if you are innocent of something that you are being accused of, then your natural reaction is to shout it from the rooftops, 'I did not do this thing!' 'What can I do to convince you? What information can I put your way to show you I didn't do what you are accusing me of doing? Here is my return ticket to Mars, here are credit card receipts from my time there, etc.' This is especially the case in rape investigation because of the stigma attached. I will never understand why a solicitor thinks it is good advice to tell him to go no comment in circumstances where their client believes they are innocent, or for that matter, why anyone would accept that advice. If you are innocent, give me the information, and I will investigate and hopefully come to that conclusion.

The idea that anyone would say, 'I didn't do it, but why should I help police? They can find out for themselves.' Surely, it is they who are being inconvenienced. The allegation of rape is a stigma upon the person accused. I have known people say that they will admit to murder before rape. I actually interviewed someone who told me that he was not a very nice person, that he burgled people's houses, dealt drugs, and he made people's lives a misery, but he would never rape a woman. In fact, I was aware of the fact in his case because we already had overwhelming evidence to show that he was innocent—evidence that had been obtained while he was in custody. It was actually my contention that he should have been released forthwith, but I was instructed to interview him. I did this very quickly and released him within an hour. I actually took him home!

This is why we would immediately think that if you do not answer reasonable questions, then you are probably guilty. In the same way, if you were there but did not do it, why would you not say so? You still have the choice of no comment, lie, or tell the truth. But what would be the point of taking the first two options if this is the truth of the matter? Why take the rap for what someone else has done unless you fear that person more than a lengthy period in prison? Even if you say, 'I was there, but I didn't do it. I don't know the person, but I can describe what happened. My DNA won't be found anywhere near.' Surely, this would be better than no comment and giving the police the belief that he may be hiding something, and is he guilty.

This leaves that last scenario. Personally, if I were guilty of anything (not that I ever would be, I hasten to add), I wouldn't answer questions. Once again, you have the same three options. You could tell the truth, but what if Old Bill do not have the evidence? You would be digging your own grave. That would be silly. You could lie, but you won't know what the officer knows, and you could trip yourself up. Once you commit yourself to a story, it is difficult to extricate yourself. Go no comment; you have nothing to lose.

What about solicitors? It helps police when there are solicitors there because the suspect cannot then say, 'I didn't know what was happening. I was confused. The nasty policeman confused me'. But we all know that the solicitors, or most of them, don't care about their clients. They see a rape case, and the first thing they think of is crown court and loads of money. Big earner. So they don't want you to admit anything.

As controversial as it may be, the only time you would need a solicitor is if you wanted to lie. I remember watching some American comedy series in the seventies. The arch villain wanted advice from his solicitor. The solicitor started telling him what he could do. The villain cut him off in mid flow and told him that he did not need a solicitor to tell him what he *could* do. He could read that in a book. He needed to know what he could get away with. If you are not going to answer questions, you don't need a solicitor. You just don't answer the questions. If you are going to tell the truth, you don't need a solicitor. The truth is what it is. It doesn't matter which angle I come from, if you are telling the truth, the account isn't going to change.

Obviously, a solicitor can't advise you to lie. Indeed, if they know you are lying, they should tell you that they can no longer represent you. At the end of the day, the only thing that a solicitor is going to do for you is to make sure your stay is at least three hours longer than it would otherwise have been. They do not ensure you get bail; they do not control the interview. It is nothing like you see on television. In fact, if any solicitor acted like they do on many detective programmes, I would have them excluded for the interview. They cannot answer questions on behalf of the suspect or interrupt unless the questioning is inappropriate. Their only role is to advise the client, nothing more.

All interviews are taped anyway, so we are not likely to be overbearing or ask inappropriate questions. Some interviews are even video recorded—a development that I think is excellent. I only wish that they would play the video in court, so the jury could see just what they get up to in interview. The smug grins, the bored looks, the off-handed attitude that so many have. I suppose that court is not supposed to be a popularity contest, but if a jury is going to make a decision on the very livelihood of someone, it would be good for them to have an idea of how he ticks.

If a solicitor is involved, then I would talk to him/her first. I have to disclose the grounds for arrest, where he was arrested, and very little else. All the information that I, by law, have to disclose can be found on the custody records. That being said, it is deemed only fair that if I want to ask questions about an event, I should at least tell them when and where it happened. It is a matter for me as the interviewing officer to decide how much I disclose and when I disclose it. Solicitors will have you believe that they need as much information as you have. In my view, you cannot test an account if you allow the suspect to know everything that you know. All he will do is work a story out around the facts. Keep some information back, and you are in a stronger position.

When all is said and done, if the suspect is telling the truth, then he will have nothing to fear. The account can be properly tested to his advantage. These are significant times in the lives of people. They will not need to be prompted that much. There is no need to tell them who may or may not have seen them or what property may have been left, or, for that matter, what fingerprints or DNA they may or may not have deposited. If it didn't happen, then it would not have been a significant part of their lives; but then they didn't do it, so why would they be interested in anything other than showing that whatever our evidence, they are not a part of the problem?

The interview takes on a similar form to the victims. So we develop the story. There are no trick questions. The questions are only tricky if you are lying. When we ask these questions of a victim, we are aware that they are volunteering that information. They do not have to remain with you. They are free to go. When we ask the questions of a suspect, under most circumstances they are not there voluntarily. The way we test the accuracy of their account is to withhold information. We have to give them a certain amount by law, but we do not have to explain away the evidence that we have.

Generally, we tell them when it is alleged to have happened, where it happened, what happened in fairly basic terms, and to whom it happened, especially when parties are known to each other. We would not, for example, tell them that we have found property belonging to him at the scene or that there are witnesses or video evidence. In this way, if they talk, we ask questions—lots of questions. We develop the account. We do not challenge that account initially in the same way as the victim. If they are telling the truth, any other evidence we have will be explained away without them even knowing they are doing it. If they are lying, we simply develop the lie. We get them to nail their colours to the mast so that there is no going back. Then later on, often in a separate interview, after he has committed himself to his account, we confront him with the evidence and watch them squirm.

An investigation that I was involved in demonstrated the advantage of this very well. The allegation was that he had been in a bus. He was drunk. In the bus were two young women, both of whom were trying to avoid him. One woman got off, and the victim was alone with the male. She alighted at the next stop. He got off with her and frogmarched her into a nearby recreation ground where he tried to rape her. She had the wherewithal to persuade him to stop what he was doing and come back to her home, which was a very short distance away. She managed to get in the house, leaving him outside, and called police. He was arrested.

In the park, he had removed some of her clothing including her socks. Where, by design or mistake, when she gathered her clothing up, she dropped a sock. We found the sock and didn't tell him. He explained that she was all over him. She was drunk and didn't want to walk home and could he take her home. He reluctantly agreed. He walked down the footway on the opposite side of the park with her hanging on to his arm. They did not go anywhere near the park, they stuck to that route. When she got home, her boyfriend stormed out of the house, hit her, and dragged her inside. We spent about three-quarters of an hour developing the part of his account that took him nowhere near the park. He was happy to talk to us and came across as a reasonable guy out and about one Friday night. He was allowed to sleep, as it was close to midnight, and we returned the next morning.

We confirmed what he had said the previous night. We then produced the sock with the information that the victim was wearing matching socks when she got off the bus. When she spoke to police and handed over all the clothing, one sock was missing. Bearing in mind the park had been secured from thirty minutes after the incident, and no one had been in or out of it in that time, how did her missing sock end up in the park? At this point, he leant forward, put his forehead onto the desk, and said in a monotone, 'I don't want to answer any more questions.' In fact, his whole account was a fabrication, and we were able to discount pretty much every aspect of it by basic investigative techniques. 'Gotcha' moments like that are few and far between and are to be savoured.

One of the tricks up many a solicitor's sleeve is the prepared statement. A solicitor is not allowed to interfere with an interview unless the police are being overbearing or aggressive or they are going off the subject. They cannot answer questions on behalf of the suspect or prevent questions being asked. What happens is that when a man is arrested, he is given the opportunity of calling a solicitor if he wants. That solicitor is called to the police station, and the interviewing officer discloses to him/her some of the basics. The solicitor is then allowed time to consult with his client. The advice he can give his/her client is either give an account and answer questions, don't answer any questions, or give a prepared statement. Solicitors like this because they can control what is being said.

A solicitor can't advise anyone to lie. If the detainee admits the offence to him, then he, by law, can only advise 'no comment' or admit everything. In fact, this is impossible to enforce, as no one is privy to the consultation. The confidentiality between solicitor and client is sacrosanct. So between client and solicitor, they work out what information they want to give to police, write it down, and then answer no further questions. This statement can be as simple as 'I neva done nuffin' to a fairly full explanation. They are ostensibly done if the solicitor is worried that the detainee is easily confused and questioning would confuse matters. They can also say that their client cooperated by giving an account when it gets to court. So a statement can say that he refutes the allegation, that any sexual contact was consensual, and in fact the victim was making all the moves. My job is then to develop this story. If it is true, he should be able to give all sorts of information about who they were with when she was coming on to him, what was being said, who removed whose clothing, was a condom used, and who put it on.

There are hundreds of questions that can firm up any account. Of course, if the client refuses to answer, we can't develop it. If he then drags someone into court to say that she was all over him, we have the opportunity to say, 'Why didn't you tell us about this witness in the first place?' Is it because he was unaware of the scenario and needed to be coached before police could get to him? So prepared statements can and do backfire.

I recall one instance when a 17-year-old oik was arrested and interviewed over the rape of someone whom he knew. The boy could barely string two words together. Not because he had a mental issue, but he had just not bothered to go to school and had spent his formative years thieving off others and sticking two fingers up to society. When I first read his statement, I saw that it was five lines long. It was bullet-pointed and each line proclaimed his innocence. I started off by confirming that it was his statement and that he agreed with everything in the statement. To which he replied, 'No comment.' (Smirk)

I had already noticed that the statement contained sentences that could only have come from someone who had a reasonably advanced knowledge of the English language. There was certainly no way that the boy in front of me would have strung those words together. I then proceeded to go through his statement word by word, phrase by phrase, and then sentence by sentence, asking if he understood what each word meant and what the word would mean in the context of the sentence. He had not a clue. The solicitor looked more and more embarrassed as time went on. Although he didn't answer my questions, I was able to make a nonsense of the statement. Because it was a written document, they could not change it, and he eventually did not contest the case.

FORENSIC SCIENCE

There is a lot of myth and misunderstanding about this subject. Everyone is expert because of CSI whatever. Forensic science can only prove one thing and one thing only in the context of the work I do: person X was in place Y at some point before the item or person or whatever is being examined was first taken into the control of police. Even then, it is not a given. For example, person smokes a cigarette. He nonchalantly flicks it away after he has finished. The butt lands in a stolen car unknown to him. Rodney Robber drives the car off and dumps it in Birmingham where it is discovered. Ida, the IDO, and Sandy, the SOCO, turn up to the stolen car and retrieve the cigarette. It is sent off to the lab, and he is identified. Need I say more?

There is no such thing as a DNA string specific to rapists. The fact that sperm is found in the intimate swabs of a woman only means that he has probably had sex with her at some point in the recent past. It is for the police to show whether or not that sex was with or without consent. It helps if the donator of the sperm has denied sex. This is unlikely for reasons previously explained. The proof lies in the circumstances.

Forensic science covers a multitude of sins. As I am an expert in nothing, I cannot give expert evidence. This means that even if I had a good understanding of computers and discovered something within the computer, I cannot use this in evidence. It has to be 'forensically' extracted. That expert can then give evidence of how he obtained the information and will be able to show that the data was not corrupted in any way. This means that anything I do in an investigation that involves anything scientific or technological has to go to the lab. Even if I was investigating a murder where the person has been decapitated, I cannot evidence the fact that the person was dead because I am not an expert.

The Met police scientists were leaders in their field around the world. Unfortunately, budgets mean more than the safety and welfare of the citizens, so the powers that be dumped the forensic science service. All those experts have now been whisked up by private companies who now charge a fortune for doing the same stuff. The biggest disadvantage is there will now be no coherent forensic science development anymore, and no standardised way of dealing with forensic science. A short-sighted and very expensive move by our hallowed leaders, I think.

Of course, with the new way of dealing with things come extra paperwork and a chance for bureaucrats. Bear in mind that they do 'forensic' exams. When they come up with results, they send us a 'report'. If the case goes to court, I will need a statement from them because the report is not sufficient. All statements have to be signed with a certificate saying that everything hereinafter is true, etc. The report will not have that certificate, so I then have to put in another application for them to do the statement. Why they can't just do the statement alongside the report is not a mystery. It just means they can't charge us again.

A scientist will never hand you a report that has the effect of a smoking gun. Everything is shrouded in maybes and likelies, so they will say things like, 'The swab from the face of the victim was analysed and amylase was detected.' This is the substance that is found in all bodily fluids but is most concentrated in saliva. The amylase was examined, and DNA was extracted. The DNA was positively compared with person X. Although amylase is most concentrated in saliva, it is also found in other bodily fluids, so it is not possible to say blah, blah, blah'. Effectively, you are given the proverbial smoking gun, then told the smoke does not mean the gun was definitely fired. We don't have a 'rape DNA'. Just because semen is found in an intimate swab, it does not mean that a rape has happened. It only means that it is likely that this man had sex with this woman at some time before the sample was extracted. It is for me to work out whether this was done consensually or not.

There are times when the evidence provided by forensic scientist hits the nail on the head—the time when I had to interview five people for an allegation of a nasty gang rape in a park. Four gave accounts when interviewed. One refused to answer questions. The park had been thoroughly searched by specialist search teams, and various condom wrappers were found. One in particular matched the description of a wrapper that the victim described. A fingerprint was lifted from the wrapper, and whose print do we think it might have been? You guessed it—the idiot who refused to answer the questions. My first job was to put them all in the park. All the ones that gave an account had done that for me. Without his account, I could not place the last one in the park, and there was a possibility that we would have insufficient evidence against him. Gotcha.

Telephones and computers offer a whole vast area of possibilities. Anything contained in a phone or computer has to be forensically extracted. But the eggheads at the lab can do wonders. When you delete something from your computer, it does not just disappear into cyberspace. All you are doing in pressing that delete button is to tell the computer that the space on the disc where that information is being held can be used and overwritten. If the computer uses that space for the next bunch of data that it receives, then that information is gone. Until that happens, it remains on the disk. Phones these days are mini computers and work in exactly the same way.

There are plenty of checks and balances when it comes to accessing telephone data. We can go through the telephone company and ask for billing information. All sorts of authorities and applications and reams of paperwork have to be completed, but it can be done. This, of course, will only tell us who calls or text messages whom. It will not give us the content of the text messages or voicemails. I had a huge argument with a defence counsel because she was insisting that I obtain the content of text messages by going through the service provider until I pointed out that she would not be happy if a private company had access to every text message and voicemail she ever sent or received. I also pointed out that no private company would want to keep that amount of useless data on their system. Imagine how many text messages are sent every minute around the world. The only way we get the content of these messages is if we actually take the phone itself and have the data forensically extracted. Of course, all this was before the advent of the 'cloud'.

The other way we can use phone is by using triangulation to find the location of a telephone. The movies have this wonderful facility that they can use. They make a quick telephone call and almost immediately are told that the telephone is in the kitchen of a specific address on the second floor. Just under the breadboard. Wouldn't it be wonderful if we could do that? What actually happens after we have written war and piece about why we need to do this and have eventually received the authority, the service provider tells us the rough area that the phone is in. They do this by finding out the three telephone masts that are closest to the phone and telling us it is in that area—normally about half a square mile or so. This information is useful if the person is saying they were in Birmingham at the time, and they have had their phone on them at all times. If we find that the phone was in Hounslow, West London, that person has some explaining to do.

It is also good for checking on missing persons and such like. It came in useful when Surrey police were looking for a very vulnerable 12-year-old girl. They had done all their research and found that she was in liaison with a 21-year-old man. More research showed that the man had a telephone number. They triangulated both phones and found them to be in the same area. This, coincidentally, was the same area as the man's home address. We were able to show that both phones were at the address overnight. When we knocked on the door, we found both parties inside. He obviously had some very awkward questions to answer about having a very young girl in his home overnight.

Closely related to forensic evidence is expert evidence. As a dull, semi-educated police officer, I am not allowed an opinion at court. Until recently, we could give an opinion about the drunkenness of an individual, but the lawmakers have decided that we are too thick even to pass that opinion. Now, we have experts who can spend thirty minutes just going through their qualifications before stating the bloody obvious in a court of law and getting paid a fortune for doing it.

We often need experts. It goes without saying the DNA profiling, for example, may require a certain amount of skill. You don't need to have a doctorate to say that the massive bruise on someone's face with no other injury was caused by 'blunt trauma'. How else is a bruise caused?

Expert witnesses will sell their souls for the sound of their own voice rationalising an opinion. I actually had a case where a woman was beaten up and raped. Her facial injuries included a large number of stitches to her lip and extensive bruising throughout her face. The suspect had admitted slapping the victim once in self-defence, catching her lip with his open palm to cause the gash to her mouth. He then went on to say that she proceeded to punch herself in the face to cause all the bruises that she sustained. At court, they called on an 'expert' to give evidence. I sat there open-mouthed throughout the drivel that came out of her mouth. She claimed that because most of the bruising was on the right side of her face (inaccurate), and he was right-handed. It was unlikely that he would have landed the blows!

Apparently, right-handed people can't punch with their left hands. And clearly, she would never have thought to turn her head from side to side while struggling. This woman was a slip of a girl: 5' 2" and 7 stone if she was an ounce! No bruising to her hands either. If we get past the notion that someone could cause such extensive injuries to themselves by punching, let us then move on to the fact that one bruise was to the back of her head (apparently feasible). She even went on to say that the bruising under the victim's eyes might not be bruising at all but natural colouring or tiredness. Black eyes are apparently caused when there is blunt trauma above the eyes, and the blood flows down into the orbital area. She seemed to think that there was no such injury above the affected area. So all you people out there who were punched in the eye and ended up with a shiner, that was just tiredness.

Of course, that little gem was kicked into touch when it was pointed out that there was blunt trauma on the bridge of the nose above the eyes. Oh, and I didn't say that she based her opinions on photographs that she had seen of the injuries. She never examined her in any way. Thankfully, the jury treated her evidence with the contempt that it deserved, and he was found guilty. She was, of course, being paid by the defence to pass her opinion. I cannot, for one second, believe that a professional with the sort of experience that she had, which was impressive, would say such things and believe them. Would she have said that if she was not being paid? If the answer to that question is yes, then I am thankful she is not my GP.

I think the problem was that she was transposing the phrase 'technically could happen' into 'probably did happen'. She could technically have done each individual thing that the expert claimed with a bit of imagination and a very supple body, but not all of them together in the same instance. I have heard of people injuring themselves by deliberately bashing their heads against a brick wall. There are countless examples of self-harm. I can think of no examples in all the years I have done this job where someone has self-harmed by punching themselves in the face. We have to be realistic here. Normally, expert witnesses are not called to court. Their statements quote the obvious and are not challenged in anyway, so we are spared their ramblings.

COURT

This is where all our investigations are tested. When there is an allegation of rape, the first thing that has to happen is that the person making the allegation has to convince a response police officer. This officer is almost invariably a perfect stranger, and while he should be empathetic and professional, he will have to ensure that there is the basis of an offence. Once this is done and someone is arrested, the custody officer has to be convinced by the officer that there is sufficient evidence to remove this person's freedom even for a short period of time. If he were to authorise a person's detention without being so convinced, he could be looking at losing his job.

The inspector, then, needs to be convinced that the investigation is progressing and that his continued detention is required while those enquiries are made. Then comes the CPS who has to be convinced that there is sufficient evidence to charge so that there is a likelihood of conviction. We then go through the process of getting the case to court. There are various preliminary hearings and case progression hearing to ensure that there is a case to be answered. The defence will pick holes all over the place so that when we eventually get to court, everyone has had their two *pen'uths*. To be able to jump through all of these hoops and still get to trial despite the best efforts of the defences and the legal system must mean one thing and one thing only. The person standing in the dock is almost certainly guilty. It is just a case of whether we can convince a jury.

The jury are treated like mushrooms for the most part (kept in the dark and fed on shit). Depending on how successful the defence or prosecution barristers are, they will eventually have only the information that the judge allows them. They will not know that they have had vital information kept from them; they are just shuffled out of the court every so often in order that the people involved can have discussions about what to include and exclude. They are then shuffled back in looking more and more frustrated about delays, and they are expected to accept this. We often have this thing where the defence want to edit a recording of the victim or defendant so that the jury does not hear something they don't want them to hear.

This is generally something that has little bearing on the facts and may show the defendant in a bad light. No one is forced to say anything. They are advised that anything they say can be given in evidence. If a defendant is going to prejudice himself (if that is physically possible), then so be it. I can see that if a victim or witness says something that has nothing to do with the case and will prejudice the case, then we should take it out, but the defence will have us taking all sorts of things out.

For example, in a rape investigation, the interviewing officer has to coax out a lot of information that is very personal and often embarrassing. The interviewer, without putting words in their mouth, will make encouraging noises and gestures like 'you are doing very well' or 'I know it is difficult, but this needs to be done' or 'you are very brave', etc. The defence would have this taken out. Why? Why would they want the police officers to come across as cold and uncaring? It doesn't prejudice anything, so why take it out and leave the jury in the dark? You can be certain that they would be happy to drag up anything about the witness, whether it has anything to do with the case or not. They are even expected to! All it does is create an uneven playing field in which the prosecution can be pilloried, and the defendant gets left alone.

I have been a juror twice, so I am in a good position to know what happens behind those doors. The only qualification that jurors need is the lack of criminal convictions. They all go on oath saying that they will make their judgement according to the evidence. Many of them ignore that oath. A juror has to come to a decision 'so that they are sure'. This means that if the jury *think* 'the evidence appears to be there, he probably did it', then they should acquit. They have to be certain. There is so much muddying of the waters in a trial where the defence will suggest to the jury that the victim had an ingrowing toenail at the time, so she was probably lying.

Even worse in rape cases, they will drag up the victim's past. They will suggest that the victim has sex with men regularly, she is therefore of a loose moral fibre, and therefore cannot be believed. If the defendant was standing there, accused of robbery, the defence would never consider suggesting that because the victim regularly used a telephone in the street, they were asking to be robbed. They would never suggest that a victim of domestic violence was to blame because she keeps going back to the abusive husband. So why do rape victims get this outrageous treatment? The legal profession are constantly trying to justify this ludicrous position, and it is they who drive this awful treatment.

It is true that rape is different to any other offence. With murder, you have a body; with theft, you have property missing; with assault, you have injury. With rape, all you have is a person who looked, sounded, and acted exactly the same before and after. This means we have to explore other avenues to try to get to the truth. This means that the prosecutors want everything on the victim. They want us to dig up their past, and they want anything that may be used against them out in the open. Their reasoning is that it is a question of who is more believable. If someone has been dishonest in the past, they could be dishonest now. I just think that the courts go over the top when it comes to digging up the past. Just because a woman has worked as a prostitute, it doesn't mean she can't be raped. Even if a woman's stated aim is to shag everything on two legs, it does not mean she can't be raped. Just because she may have lied about something in the past—let he who has not sinned cast the first stone—it does not mean she cannot be raped.

It is time to rely on the evidence and consider whose account is plausible. I know we have to prove beyond doubt, but when you get some of the cock and bull stories that we have to endure from defendants who only have to plant a seed of doubt, I think that we can look to the general public's common sense. Lord knows we can't rely on the common sense of your average judge. Most of them are not of this planet. They live a world removed from all the nastiness. I don't think they realise that the stuff they spend every working day of their lives dealing with actually does happen. It is all an academic exercise. Hypothetical situations sent to them, so they can exercise their knowledge of the law.

For all the oaths that the jury do, it is still going to be a popularity contest. If the jury like the victim, it is more likely that they will return a verdict of guilty. Beyond the popularity contest, there are also the cultural beliefs of some of the jurors. Many people don't like to hear it, but there are cultures out there that believe women should be obscene and not heard. They believe that they are there to do as they are told. If they are raped, it is their fault. If their husband forces his attentions on her, it is his right to do so, and the woman should shut up and put up. The people who believe this are not interested in the laws of this land and will apply their own beliefs. What this means is that if there are more than two jurors with this firmly held belief, there will never be a guilty verdict no matter how much evidence there is.

There are also cultures out there where the age of consent is much lower than ours. Some as low as twelve and even this line is pretty grey. The general view in some of these cultures is that if the girl is menstruating, they are legal. I am aware of one case where a 10-year-old girl was raped. There was an eyewitness in that the mother walked in on it. There was also DNA evidence to make absolutely certain. It went to trial, and the jury could not agree. It ended up a hung jury, and the trial had to be reheard using a different one. This could only be a case of at least three members of the jury thinking that the 35-years-old man's actions were perfectly reasonable. Fortunately, the second jury didn't have paedophiles in it, and he was convicted.

What I am saying is that the decision of the jury, especially when it is a verdict of not guilty but sometimes when it is one of guilty, is not always made as a result of the strength or weakness of the evidence.

This makes the whole system a mockery. When the defence goes for the character assassination of the victim, it is in the knowledge that they will not be making their decision based on evidence but on what they think of the two parties concerned. If the law banned outright information that related to the victim and the suspect's past and tried the case on the evidence, I think there would be a more level playing ground. If there was then a way of excluding people whose cultural background will dictate their decision, then we may start getting better results.

I have dealt with two cases where prostitutes were raped. These are surprisingly easy to deal with. Generally speaking, you have suspects, victims, and witnesses who have all led lives that most can't understand. They are normally not pleasant people. Prostitutes are, by and large, honest people—certainly when it comes to bodily functions—but dishonest when it comes to theft and fraud. Their pimps and customers are normally not that honest. What you *do* have is a group of people that the jury are not going to like. The popularity contest is therefore taken out of the equation, and they are left with the facts of the case— or at least the facts that the court allows them to hear. Put aside the odd person who will be of the opinion that a prostitute doesn't deserve justice. They are in the minority, and you get a verdict that reflects the facts.

I disagree with the media when they say things like 'person X appealed against his conviction, and the court found him to be innocent'. Courts do not find people innocent. They find them guilty or not guilty. In other words, the prosecution has proved the case or they have not. This does not mean he has not done it, only that we cannot prove it. Appeal courts will find convictions 'unsafe'. What they will not say is that they have looked at the evidence, and it appears that this person never did it. If I hit someone in the nose and manage to get a jury to acquit me, it doesn't mean that they have turned the clock back and undone the assault.

The most famous case is Stephen Lawrence. No one, for an instant, felt that the defendants were innocent when they were acquitted. The government even actually changed legislation to allow 'double jeopardy'.

One of the only sensible pieces of legislation change that I have seen for ages, if for no other reason than it proves this very point. It essentially means that if new information comes to light, which was not available at the time, we can retry the person. This is a facility that was not available to us before. We may never know what happened on that day. We may question the idea that it was just a bunch of thugs attacking a perfectly innocent man who was minding his own business, but we have never really questioned the fact of their guilt.

AND SO

And so what of this reluctance? Why have I enjoyed my time, and yet I can't wait until it is over? I think it is time to review the evidence. I will go through the organisation from bottom to top. I will start with the public not because they are the bottom of the pile, but just because it is more convenient. I will be ending with the press, and no one can say that a group of people who make their living out of picking through other people's rubbish bins for some bit of salacious gossip are at the top of any pile.

PUBLIC

There are two basic types of people who don't like me purely because of the job I do: criminals who find my presence inconvenient when they need to continue with their nefarious deeds, and those gullible people who believe that if it's in the newspaper, then it must be true. We are, of course, talking about the mischievous press who like to use the police as a whipping boy as a way of selling copy.

Generally, the public are very supportive and just want us to do our jobs. They are the source of our information, and they are the ones that make the job work. They are the glue that binds everything together. Yes, many seem to think that we can pluck evidence out of thin air, and many have expectations that are unrealistic, but then my expectations of other tradesmen's abilities are probably unrealistic sometimes when I don't understand their limitations.

CONSTABLES

Obnoxious, arrogant, opinionated, insensitive, and sometimes downright rude are some of the home truths that some of my colleagues need to hear. Mostly, they are honest, compassionate, caring, and with an overriding determination to get the job done regardless of how much those in charge tie our hands behind our backs, provide substandard equipment, and generally make our life difficult. I have heard many coppers complain that we are our own worst enemies because we put up with poor management and poor equipment and just make the job work. I am sure that if someone in the private sector was asked to do a job, it would get done as long as the equipment was provided. Private industry would love to scrimp on equipment, but if they are going to do it better than the next chap, they have to spend the money. Unfortunately, we have a monopoly, so the bosses can tell us to swivel when we complain.

This is a rank where you constantly have to prove yourself. Your peers want to know that they can trust you in dangerous situations. You, sergeants, don't want to clear up your mess, and the inspectors want you to make them look good. Regardless of what your career path is, you have to be sound in this rank. Every other rank will feel they know more about it than you no matter how experienced you are and how inexperienced they are. A constable will have to make decisions on the hoof all the time with no manual to study before each one. It doesn't really work so well when you say to a samurai-wielding mad man, 'Er, excuse me, before you lop that chap's head off, can you give me a sec while I read up on the SOPs for this scenario? Oops, too late.' You just have to deal with it as best you can. The inspector can expound all he likes from the comfort of his office about how he would have dealt with it if he were there at the time, but there is nothing quite like being there.

SERGEANTS

The first step up that rickety old ladder that is promotion. At this point, you are still on the streets, still doing the shifts, and you are basically a constable with some extra metalwork on your shoulder and a few extra responsibilities. If one of your subordinates screws up, you are probably going to get it in the neck just as much as the offender himself.

There are two basic types of sergeant. Those who are looking to climb all the way up that greasy pole, and those stalwarts who stay where they are. They differ in one major area: they both have to make decisions, but the stalwart will make decisions that are designed to resolve whatever situation it is he wants to resolve; the other will make decisions based on how he can evidence a particular 'skill' area in his next promotion attempt. As a rule, the fly boy would normally find himself a safe little job away from the front line, leaving our care-worn stalwarts to get on with the business of policing.

The crotchety old fart can be a real pain when he holds you up with some dogma that somehow, his way is the way, he's always done it, and that's how it is going to stay. There are some remarkably young sergeants with that attitude. The very worst sergeants are the ones that are on their way up, don't intend to be in that rank very long, and so are, by definition, inexperienced but insist on riding rough shod over your investigation—knowing that he won't have to deal with the fall out— just so that he can log his decision-making skills. You just know that if the job is ultimately successful, his report will be glorifying his role; and if it is not, he will not even acknowledge his presence there.

INSPECTORS

This is the rank where you start to drift away from policing and start moving towards management. The best inspectors are the ones who leave you to get on with your job and are there to sign the forms they need to sign and authorise what they need to authorise. But as with the sergeants, there are two types: the flier and the stalwart. The stalwart is normally a little frustrated that he hasn't been able to go further but is often comfortable with his role. The flier can be painful. This rank is one where many decisions have to be made that seriously affects the lives of others—this is serious shit here, make no mistake. Most make those decisions easily and with good knowledge of the subject he is making decisions on. The fly boy doesn't like that. His mantra is if you don't make a decision, you can't make a bad decision. If you don't make a bad decision, your promotion prospects can't be damaged. They still have to evidence decision-making in their next promotion interview, but they are now learning how to be a politician. If you make a big decision, make sure you are deniable if it goes wrong, and try to get someone else to make it if possible.

I have witnessed this cowardice at first-hand on more than one occasion. It turns my stomach! Normally, these idiots hide in some office, making decisions on which colour of ink to use in their next report, and how they are going to spin that into something that approximates an example of decisiveness for their next promotion board. Not difficult if you bear in mind that the panel who judge the promotion candidates have all been there and done the same thing.

CHIEF INSPECTORS

This is a nonsense rank. They don't have a proper role. They don't run anything, make any real decisions, or do anything of substance. It is a dying rank, and it will probably disappear altogether in the next few years. It is merely a staging post for the next real rank. Having said that, on the rare occasion that I have come across a really good one—the type that makes you see the difference between a leader and a manager—I have found that they have made for a much better working environment. I have seen plenty of bad examples, and they don't make any difference at all.

SUPERINTENDENT

This is a tough job. You are now a distance from the 'coalface'. The job is administrative for the most part, but you still have to make the decisions. Higher rank equals bigger decisions. Now, there aren't so many hiding places. The job often entails being either the senior officer of the area (Borough commander) or his second-in-command or you are heading up a major department like the murder teams or Sapphire.

That means if your station or department isn't working as well as it might, it's down to you. They get huge pressure from above to get their statistics in order. (Please note that the higher ranks don't want superintendents to sort out the crime problem or get a handle on the burgeoning gang problem. No, no! As long as they get their stats right, everything will be fine.)

The problem with all this is that shit rolls downhill. If they get it in the neck, we get it in the neck. They don't care how badly resourced we are as long as the heating in their office is working properly, and they can get us to jiggle with their stupid statistics. They have a lot of serious decisions to make that could place officers safety at risk or deprive people of some rights that the rest of us take for granted. Decisions made by these people change lives. Politicians need to understand this: superintendents also need to know that I will do the job to the best of my abilities, and I will seek out the truth. If that ruins his statistics, I couldn't care less.

UPPER ECHELONS

These are the people who no longer hold the office of constable. They are the commanders, deputy assistant commissioners, assistant commissioners, deputy commissioners, and the commissioner. I list these just to ram home how crowded the upper echelons are. How many assistants and deputies does any one man need? And what is the difference between a deputy and an assistant? As far as I can see, they all have but one aim: they are all vying for the top job that gets them a knighthood, a healthy pension, and some obscure little quango to play with in his dotage.

The current commissioner is a hatchet man who got his position by promising to start the process of breaking up the police service piece by piece so that the government can build a new one out of the rubble in its own image. At least he is good at getting his face on the telly! The problem is that they are reliant on the politicians for their ambitious aims, so they aren't going to rock any boats, lest they are thrown overboard.

LEGAL PROFESSION

<u>This,</u> in my humble opinion, is one of the most dishonest professions in the world. They don't care about their clients. If it's a major job that is likely to go to the crown court, it means money for them, so it does not pay them to have their client admitting to anything, especially if they think their client is innocent because then they get paid for the court case and get a not guilty verdict. Great for their reputation.

They are not there to get to the truth; they are there to get their clients off. Ironically, that is the one thing they will never really be able to do. Only a lack of evidence to show guilt or evidence that shows they are innocent will do that. That information will come from the investigation, not the lawyers.

The barristers care even less for the defendant. All they want to do is win the argument. They will form their own opinion as to whether the defendant is guilty, but it won't enter into their strategy. Their client is the solicitor's firm, not the defendant, and their job is to win the argument whether their argument is true or not. Judges are so removed from the real world it is laudable. They will know that if the police have managed to get a case as far as a trial at crown court with all the hoops they have to jump through, the likelihood is that the defendant is guilty. But they can't pass an opinion, that is for the jurors, so all they are left with is the academic argument.

POLITICIAN

In the last paragraph, I mentioned that I believed the legal profession to be one of the most dishonest of professions. Well, let me introduce you to the profession that is, by far and away, the most dishonest. Duplicitous, self-serving to a man (or woman) when you get to the higher echelons of the political world, they are not interested in the victims of crime and how it affects them. They are only interested in how they can manipulate the figures to demonstrate their own political standpoint. They will couch their decisions in ambiguity so that if the general incident about which they are making their decision is successful, they can embrace the whole operation as their own, and their decision will be the pivotal point that marked success from failure. If the thing fails, they can deny all knowledge and walk away, allowing one of his/her underlings to take the fall. Politicians see police as a necessary evil and a provider of statistical information. They don't help in the fight against crime and, more often than not, hinder it.

PRESS

Another group who seem to find the search for the truth a rather boring inconvenience. The police are the whipping boys because no one, especially the senior police officers, fights our corner. This means that any salacious tittle-tattle is food and drink to many rags. It seems amazing to me that when a newsworthy crime hits the newspaper and a suspect is apprehended, the press seem to convict them there and then. Some even boast having a hand in the apprehension of the villain. No such thing as innocent until proven guilty. They will also bang on about mistakes that were made in very high-profile murder cases because information was not shared between forces.

The Soham murders are prime example. They went on *ad nauseam* about how police failed to share information between forces and with the education authorities. This was never a mistake. He had never been convicted of anything, so, at the time, due to the Data Protection Act, police were not allowed to pass information on. They would have been breaking the law. The press conveniently forgot about that, and a law was quietly passed that insisted that we share information. The transition was almost seamless, so it looked like police were always allowed to share this information but we just chose not to.

Of course, then you have the 'Rough Justice' programmes. This was a television programme where some jumped up little journalist would say that they had proof that this poor chap, who had been languishing in a dungeon for thirty years, was absolutely innocent, and they meant to make a television programme to show the nasty policemen for what they are. You watch the programme, and you find that their 'proof' is just some anecdotal rubbish like some little, old granny saying, 'My grandson's mate's second cousin twice removed said he was with him all that day, so it couldn't have happened. I told the police at the time, but they wouldn't listen.' So all the evidence that a jury heard and considered was to be ignored because of not provable, disregarded information that could never be confirmed after the passage of time.

I knew some police officers who were stitched up by some aristocratic toff back in the early nineties. It was so obvious it was a stitch-up. There were holes in the evidence you could drive a train through. When they went to the Rough Justice programme makers, they weren't interested, and they were quite plain about why—the victim of the rough justice were police officers.

I saw a programme on television the other day where they demonstrated how people would follow the crowd because of our pack instinct. They had about five stooges and one member of the public and were all asked questions in each other's presence and hearing. The stooges were instructed to get some very easy questions wrong. They were all to give the same incorrect answer in each case. The member of the public was placed strategically at the end of the line and asked the same question. On each occasion, she gave the same incorrect answer. It was very revealing, but it also demonstrates why journalists will go on TV and say things like 'most people agree that . . .' and then give some opinion that I, for one, do not agree with. By saying 'most people', they are manipulating public opinion in my view. They are suggesting that if 'most people' think this and you don't, then you are the one with the problem.

Unfortunately, many people fall into this trap and agree with the statement. I wonder what would happen if they just made the statement without prefixing it with 'most people'. I would not be surprised if the opinion differ. The press are a very powerful entity, and they could do to be more responsible.

ME

Despite this tirade, I am not a whinger. I get on with it. All I ask is that I am allowed to do my job. I get my satisfaction from the public's thanks when I get it right. I like the fact that I have been directly responsible for removing some nasty and dangerous individuals from society and thereby making other people's lives that little bit better. I like that I am allowed to make the important decisions. My supervisors are always happy to rubber-stamp the decisions when they have to because I haven't given them cause to worry.

I hate the fact that the entire system seems to be set-up to implode on itself at any time. The people who should be there to hold it all together are the architects of the organisation's failings. The people who should be ripping it apart—the criminals—seem to be the ones holding it together. It's nonsense, and I have had enough.

When it all comes down to it, I can say that the people who I work directly with are, by and large, good people who are easy to get on with, like-minded, and hard-working. They make the job what it should be. The vast majority of decent, hard-working people outside the police, who come to us only as a last resort and genuinely want us to help them, make me feel that I want to pull all the stops. When a job is successfully resolved for those people, and they show their appreciation by a shake of the hand or just a thank you, the job seems worth it and I want to come to work. If it was just those people who I had to deal with, then there would be no reluctance.

Unfortunately, politics is ubiquitous. The people who peddle this horrible self-serving attitude are omnipresent. Those outside the immediate environs of the job who take pleasure in putting barriers in the way of those of us who just want to get to the truth are out there in their droves. It is they who are responsible for this 60,000-word, 460-paragraph rant!

Before and After

As I write this, I am drawing to the end of my career in the police. It has been a career that has served me well but has changed out of all recognition. This chapter deals with those changes and asks the question, 'Is this change for the better of just political manoeuvrings?' Basically, this is the bit where I bang on about 'those halcyon days'. The kids these days, they haven't the sense they were born with, wouldn't know a hard days work if it kicked them up the backside, etc.

Before

When I started, in Hendon uniform meant just that. Everyone wore the same. A hat was worn when outside but removed when inside. When we moved as a group or class, we marched in close formation. When we passed a senior officer, we saluted sharply. The uniform was quite smart and was fire-resistant but definitely *not* weather-resistant.

After

Now, Hendon is all but decommissioned. Police recruits get 'on-the-job training', which means they don't get any training, or the police who are training them are not qualified instructors and are passing on their own lack of knowledge. They all seem to be wearing different clothes that they manage to call 'uniform'. I am, however, told that it is more weatherproof than it used to be. The problem is that it is all synthetic material that is never going to be fireproof. I'll take the weather any day if it protects me just once against a firebomb.

Before

Hendon was never a place where one learned to be police officers—although some instructors did believe that. It was there to provide you with the tools with which to carry out your duty. We learned legislation in parrot fashion because when you are out on the street scratching your head over something that you have bumbled into, by knowing the elements of the law, you can start to pick the bones out of the situation. Hendon taught us that. What they could not teach us is how to calm down a potentially violent situation nor could they teach us how to resolve a neighbour dispute. That was just down to experience and interpersonal skills.

Coppers still have that, but they do not have the basic knowledge. I would like to think that Hendon was also there to try to identify the ones who were there for the wrong reasons, but I don't think so. 'If you can't do, teach' applied in spade loads at Hendon. The instructors were never any kind a street copper, they wanted the quiet life with no prospect of overtime. They would not know a bad egg if he was walking around with a sign on his back! They were there to teach the legislation; demonstrate, as far as they could, how to apply it; and ram home the importance of being honest and level-headed.

After

What's Hendon? Even when Hendon was a going concern, towards the end, recruits were mooching around in different uniforms, wearing hats occasionally, and being taught stuff that we had to unteach when they came into the real world. The new recruits were told that other PCs were of the same rank and therefore could not tell them what to do. They translated that into not listening to anything the older officers had to say and thereby not learning from their experience. I am fully aware that there are many people out there who are very experienced and still rubbish at their jobs, but it doesn't take long to find them out and take advice from people who are best placed to give it.

Before

When I was eventually released onto an unsuspecting public, I walked the beat for several years. In my area, there were three police vehicles on each shift: an unmarked GP vehicle, a marked van with a blue light, and an area car with a blue light and two tones. Most areas would have run a 'panda' car, which was a marked Ford Fiesta with no siren and often no blue light. In my area, we just used the unmarked car. No one could drive any police vehicles until they had undergone a four-week standard driving course, which allowed you to drive police cars without blue lights or two tones. You couldn't drive the van until you had done that course plus a two-day van course. You couldn't even walk past the area car until you had done a further six-week advanced course.

After

When I eventually got the chance to become a driver, it had changed. The standard course was now a three-week response course, which allowed you to drive car with blue lights and two tones. On the course, they started with the fact that when we first learn to drive, we use a three-point system: mirror, signal, manoeuvre. They taught a six-point system; therefore, it was much better, which it was. I am not sure how they justified 'improving' that system by changing it to a five-point system, but in the best traditions of the Met police farce, they did it.

Still Later

Now, anyone can drive a police car after a five-minute check test and will be driving what the old standard drivers used to drive. Admittedly, they can't use red lights as a give way in emergencies or break the speed limit, but they can drive the cars now. The response course is two weeks instead of four and includes the van course. The area car course is three or four weeks instead of six. They will insist that they have improved driver training. Yeah, right! Then, of course, as soon as you make a mistake on the road—brought on by pressures from above to get to calls five minutes before they have come out—they prosecute you for dangerous driving. This means points on your own private driving licence and not some special police licence. They don't do that.

I will personally never drive a marked police car in anger again. I never went for the advanced course for the same reason and never will. Yes, I know, police people are human; and as such, there are some idiot drivers around, but any amount of training has to do some good.

Before

When I started out, it was considered a disciplinary offence to come to work in ill health. The reasons seem obvious to us: they did not want others to pick up whatever lurgy was floating around in the atmosphere. If you came to work with the flu and everyone came down with the same two weeks later, your selfishness would cause an entire shift to go off sick potentially. Of course, there were plenty of people who would take the piss. We had a very generous deal that we would not lose any pay while off sick. There are people out there who strung it out for years before coming back to work. Clearly, this was not a good idea and had to be changed.

After

So they did. At first, it was fine, and people couldn't stay away from work long-term without consequences—normally financial. And if they were off for over a year, they would have to justify remaining on the payroll. Fantastic for people like me who didn't go off sick. Then, of course, they got bold. The sick record would be pulled out if you wanted to transfer and used against you. That is fine, but what if it is genuine illness like a broken leg? It can take you out for months and even have a year before you are properly fit. Should one be penalised for that regardless of how well they do their job? I think not. What if the injury was caused in the line of duty? If it meant that you would probably never get back to full fitness, then that is a tragedy but unavoidable. But if you are likely to get back to full fitness, why should you be penalised?

It goes further though. I believe it is happening in all industry, but essentially, it comes down to this. Twenty years ago, if you stubbed your toe on a paving stone, they would book you off sick for as long as you wanted. Not only was your toe fully heeled when you returned, but the person also appeared to have obtained a fantastic tan and a credit card bill to their local travel agency. Several years later, when the numpties in NSY worked it all out, they changed the rules so that if you stubbed your toe on a paving stone, they would apply first aid, make every effort to get you back to work, supply physio where necessary, and advise you about civil claims in case you wanted to blame the council on your own stupidity.

Time passed, and the powers that be realised that they were running out of money (at least that is what they were told). The effect was that they had to get rid of people. Now, if you stub you toe on a paving stone, they arrest you, charge you with criminal damage to council property (the paving stone), and fire you as a criminal.

Before

Superintendents were these really scary all-powerful creatures that you treated with the utmost reverence. The CID was some sort of ethereal entity that no one really knew about. Even if one had an inkling, one would not know how to handle them in any case. They were a law unto themselves, apparently as dodgy as the day was long and also had a bottle of whisky in their drawers, which they drank from before going out to drive police cars to the local pub to speak to some phantom informant. They dealt with high-end protracted criminal investigations. They took no shit from anyone other than the DI and the DCI from whom they took plenty. They were expected to work all hours god sent but were paid plenty of overtime.

After

This is mostly urban myth (except for the overtime), although I don't doubt that there were incidents. Now, superintendents are, by and large, officers who have been shoved up the rank structure so quickly that they have no clue about what we—much less they—do for a living. As a result, they have become contemptuous taskmasters who are making people do things for no other reason than to advance their own career prospects. From the CID perspective, superintendents are only there to rubber stamp decisions that can only be made by that rank or above. But they *are* expected to rubber stamp the decisions because those of us who are asking for them, know what we are doing better than they.

The CID are now seen as a whipping boy of the Met. All the troubles are dumped on them so that if blame is to be apportioned, the CID will get it. Now, they are told to deal with everything from neighbours bleating about where they are allowed to put their dustbins, right the way up to robbery and attempted murder. They are expected to work all hours god sends and are whinged at if they are claiming for too much overtime.

Before

Adult criminals had a guarded respect for the Old Bill, but kids were rude, violent, whingeing horrors who would take anything that was not bolted down, and would bleat anytime things wouldn't go their own way.

After

Adult criminals have a guarded respect for the Old Bill, but kids are rude, violent, whingeing horrors who would take anything that was not bolted down, and would bleat any time things wouldn't go their own way. Some things never change.

Before

The Police and Criminal Evidence (PACE) Act of 1984 came into power just before I started. This was a new way of governing police powers to stop and search and to arrest. Because it was so far-reaching, the trainers at Hendon put the fear of God into all of us considering searching or arresting anyone. Taken literally, the act would effectively stop police officers doing anything at all, so it took a little time to bed in.

After

Nowadays, the bosses put the fear of God into us if we aren't stopping everyone at least twice a day and arresting everyone who treads on the cracks in the pavement. The reason? Stop and search and arrests create statistics, and statistics get bosses all excited.

Before

When I started, if a call came out, we would assess whether it required a 'blue light run' or something less urgent. It wasn't rocket science. If it was to an accident involving serious injury, you got there quick. If there was a fight, you got there quick but made sure your sirens were blaring so that the sensible ones would skedaddle before we got there. Anyone stupid enough to still be there would get scooped up. If there was a suspect on premises, you would get there quick, but you wouldn't want to alert them of your presence, so it would be a silent approach wherever possible. If it was a shoplifter, you got there when you got there.

After

Then some bright spark decided to standardise calls so that the decision-making was taken away from the practitioners and given to some shiny arsed civvie sitting in an office at NSY. If an officer with local knowledge thought that a call needed an urgent response because of something that was not made obvious by the caller—something that he had prior knowledge of—he would have to get the call upgraded. Then the blue lights would come on, and off he would go like the world was going the other way. It did not matter what the call was as long as it was an 'I' (immediate response) call.

Because the decision-making was taken away from them, all 'immediate' or 'I graded calls' were done on a blue light run so that they warned the villains of their approach and gave them time to get away. When you had a go at the driver for scaring away a burglar, they would look at you as if you were senile. 'I' call equals blue light! It seemed that they were more interested in the driving to the call rather than dealing with the problem in the best way.

Before

If you wanted to find out about a certain person or premises, I would wander into the collator's office. The collator was normally a crusty, old copper who had been around the block more times than he would admit. He would normally be the font of all local knowledge, and he would collate all incoming intelligence. A fifteen-minute chat every day went a long way, and you could flick through the files of all the local thugs to see what they were up to. He would often have some sort of assistant, and he was almost always a 'he'. So you would, for example, walk in and say, 'I saw Billy Burglar yesterday. He was walking with Rodney Robber in Toffsville Street.'

'Ah', says the collator, 'there has been a few break-ins around there recently! What was he wearing?' Suddenly, from a passing conversation, you are on your way to clearing up a series of burglaries. It was a good system, and it worked.

After

Now, they have a computerised intel system. They have a whole department with a DI, several DSs, DCs, and civilian staff, all collating information coming in on this wonderful new tool. There is no one with local knowledge, no one who talks to the street coppers, and the intel is rubbish. It is all two weeks out of date. There is so much useless information that you have to wade through to get to the juicy bit that you can't see the wood for the trees.

An old colleague of mine used to come to work and spend fifteen minutes going through all the intel at the beginning of the shift. While he was out and about, he would visit the addresses that he felt were of interest. He would stop and talk to whoever was there, then go on to the next place. Within six months of him working in that area, his knowledge of the ground was so superior to the computer intel system that we would just bypass it and go straight to him. His intel was up-to-dote and accurate. The bosses never saw what was happening and refused to change their ways, so we still have the same ol' out of date information that everyone swears by.

Before

If a superintendent wanted to dish out a bollocking, you would be summoned to the office where he would tear a strip off you.

After

Now, they hide in their offices and email the DCI who emails the DI who emails the DS who then politely tells you that you may have slipped up at some point in the distant past.

There you have it. I could go on and on about this subject, but I hope it demonstrates that those halcyon days were not always as halcyon as some would like you to believe, but some of the old methods had their place, and we have lost our way since their demise. The Met seems to want to change for the sake of change, and in so doing, it destroys some good working practises. Ironically, when something desperately needs to change because something has gone horribly wrong, they dither and procrastinate and try to get other people to make the decision just in case their decision is wrong.

For some time, I have believed that if someone wants to get promotion, when he/she is interviewed, the interviewer should ask this question: 'What was your biggest cock-up, and what did you learn from it?' Most senior management spent their time avoiding making decisions because if you don't make a decision, you can't make a bad one and your career can't be adversely affected. I believe that if we learn by our mistakes, and you have a candidate who has never made a mistake, he has never learned anything.

The answer to the question should never be, 'Oh, I forgot to sharpen my pencil this morning, so my writing was slightly unclear. I have learned by this mistake.' If the interviewer gets this response, the interview should be over, and the candidate should be told to go and do something for a living or be more honest. Because the candidate would either have been hiding under his desk his entire career or he would have been lying to the board. Either way, he has to fail. The response has to show not only that you make the big decisions but also that you accept the responsibility when it goes wrong, and you are not afraid to admit it and learn from it.

Glossary of Acronyms and Jargon

This list is not exhaustive, but it shows how the hierarchy love alphabet soup.

AFO	Authorised Firearms Officer (never, never, never)
ARB	(See CARB) Accident Report Book
BD	Kensington
BFM	Borough Forensic Manager
BOCU	Borough Organisation Command Unit (Fancy name for police division.)
CAD	Computer-Aided Despatch (Obsolete commuter system rejected by London airports)
CAIT	Child Abuse Investigation Team (I hate this acronym. CPT or child protection team always seemed more appropriate)
CARB	Collision/Accident Report Book
CID	Criminal Investigation Department
CIPP	Criminal Investigation Prosecution and P (CID) (No one knew what the last P was even when we used the acronym regularly.)

CPS	Crown Prosecution Service (Never saw them prosecuting any crowns.)
CPT	See CAIT
Crimint	Criminal Intelligence (oxymoron)
CRIS	Crime Reporting Information System
CSE	Child Sex Exploitation
CSM	Crime Scene Manager (They liked to think they managed the scene but always deferred to me when it came to closing it.)
CSU	Community Safety Unit (No earthly reason to call it this. They deal with domestic violence.)
DC	Detective Constable (me)
DCI	Detective Chief Inspector (a dying rank)
DCS	Detective Chief Superintendent (normally the top Johnny Banana at police stations)
DFS	Digital Forensic Service (computers and such like—not fingers)
Digi Pen	Digital Penetration (by fingers, not computers)
DI	Detective Inspector (nuff said)
DNA	Deoxyribonucleic Acid
DPA	Data Protection Act (the most misunderstood piece of legislation)
DSu	Detective Superintendent
DSU	Divisional support Unit (Now TSG)
DPS	Department of Professional Standards
DoI	Department of information
DASH	A set of question to victims of domestic assaults (I think it stands for Domestic and Sexual Health.)
EAB	Evidence Assessment Book (just a notebook)
Emerald	Wanted/Missing persons database
F&R	Finance and Resources Team (They didn't want the full acronym—no humour)
FH	Hammersmith and Fulham

FSS	Forensic Science Service
G&P	Grip and Pace (sort of control room)
IC	Identification Code
ID	Heathrow Airport
IDO	Identification Officer (See SOCO or CSE or CSM or whatever someone else cooks up in the name of promotion.)
IIP	Integrated Intelligence Package (For years, we had a dozen different databases, none of which spoke to each other. This tried to remedy that.)
INFOS	Cross agency intelligence checking system
IO	Investigating Officer (see OIC)
IRB	Incident Report Book (old style EAB and probably etymologically more accurate)
Jigsaw	RSO monitoring unit
Lid	Uniformed Police Officer (Derog)
LOB	Load Of Bollox
LX	Brixton
LS	Streatham
MAPPA	Multi Agency Planning and Protection Arrangements
MERLIN	Missing Persons Reporting System
NCS	National Crime Service (SOCA, as was. Clearly changing the name has made all the difference)
NSPIS	The computerised custody record (Not a clue what it stands for, but the CPS has a completely different system by the same name.)
OIC	Officer in the Case (The only time I will have letters after my name.)
PACE	Police and Criminal Evidence Act
PC	Police Constable
PNC	Police National Computer (where all the criminals are to be found)

PND	Police National Database (a not-very-good attempt at joined up thinking across police forces in the UK)
PolCol	Collision involving a police car (even if the police car wasn't physically involved)
PPU	Public Protection Unit (missing persons)
PPV	Prisoner Property Voucher
PR	Personal Radio
PS	Police Sergeant
QA	Harrow
Q car	Unmarked response car
QK	Kilburn
RA	Risk Assess
RASSO	Rape and Sexual Assault Office (CPS)
Rat	Uniformed traffic officer (they even call themselves that)
RIPA	Regulatory Investigation Procedures Act (surveillance issues)
RSO	Registered Sex Offencer
Sapphire	Sexual Offences Investigation Unit
SCD	Serious Crime Directorate (not sure if this is a directorate for serious crime or a crime directorate that is serious)
SC&O	Serious Crime and Operations (SCD as was)
SIO	Senior Investigating Officer (they don't investigate but they are often senior)
SMT	Senior Management Team (Why do senior police ranks think they are managers? In the world outside the Met, they couldn't manage a piss-up in a brewery.)
SNT	Safer Neighbourhood Team (home beat officers as was)
SOIT	Sexual Offences Investigation Techniques

SQ	Single Quarters (aka 'The Square'. These existed up until the early nineties)
STU	Safer Transport Unit
SOCO	Scenes of Crime Officer (IDO or CSE or CSM, etc.)
TSG	Territorial Support Group (lots of alternatives reflecting their 'my gang is bigger than yours' attitude)
TW	Twickenham
Twos and Blues	Emergency run in a marked police car
UTU	Uniform Tasking Unit
Viido	Video Unit (someone can't spell)
VK	Kingston
VW	Merton
WA	Battersea
WW	Wandsworth
XA	Acton
XH	Hounslow
ZA	Addington
ZD	Croydon
ZT	Sutton

Again, this is not exhaustive, but no one would bat an eyelid if they overheard a telephone conversation that went something like, 'Hi, is this the CAD room? Can I have a PNC on an IC1 suspect? NSPIS number ABC123 I'm am CSU at QA. Required for SIO debrief and SNT briefing re DASH.'

Makes perfect sense!

AUTHOR'S NOTE

*T*he following passage was written circa 2011. It was a reaction to a lot of political machinations at the time, particularly to do with the relationship between the politicians, the police, and the press. It is a work of fiction, but feel free to draw what comparisons you feel appropriate. A lot of water has passed under the bridge, and the political landscape in this respect has not settled.

A Fetid Stench

To end all this, let me regale you with a story. This is a story that, on the surface, is one of a businessman getting too big for his boots and getting knocked down to size. The more one thinks about it, though, the more the fetid stench of political manoeuvrings seems to rise up and infect the entire sorry mess.

Let us make this absolutely clear. This is a fictional account, and one that is the product of my own imagination. We must remember that most fiction will use real situations as inspiration or as a backdrop for their storytelling. This is no different to that. Some people may read this and draw parallels to current situations. I have no personal knowledge of the political current affairs, only what I read in the newspapers, and we know how they can distort facts. Any parallels that are drawn are done at the reader's own risk. I cannot take responsibility for other people's wild imagination.

Once upon a time, there was an Australian—shall we call him Winfred (Winnie to his friends) Paddington—who decided that he would quite like to own a newspaper. Being a pushy sort, he got his way and worked his way up the international hierarchy within the media world. Eventually, he got so high that he bashed his head on the proverbial glass ceiling and found that he could rise no further. Not being one to accept such barriers, he decided to break the glass ceiling (glass is good like that—very brittle and easy to break).

Having got past this barrier, he continued to rise until he was the most powerful media mogul in the world and found, once again, that he could rise no further. Again, these sorts of barriers annoy him. He now spends his time working out how to get more. What does one do when one has all that power? Look for more, obviously! What does one do when you own three-quarters of the media? Aim for all of it, obviously. If you aim for the moon and only get halfway, you are nowhere. If you aim for the stars and only get halfway . . .

Now, there are a lot of very powerful people out there that politicians either do not worry about or who they actively associate with. Tiny Rowlands of Lonrho in the seventies and eighties and Oppenheimer of Anglo American were two prime examples. There are many current examples today. Politicians are happy with these people. They employ, they create wealth, they grease palms, and everyone is happy. Okay, they may be a little shady, and some of the ways they do things are not always morally correct. But as long as no one is getting hurt—or at least if they are, it is the wronguns that get it—then who is going to argue?

The media, on the other hand, is another story. If all the media were of one mind, they could change governments just by bombarding the newspapers and TV with negativity. The media is always powerful, but there must be some way of creating balance. In the media, that is by making sure that they all have differing agenda. If one person was to have a controlling influence and therefore one agenda, checks and balances are lost.

There isn't a politician in the world that would accept this, so when our Aussie started making moves to take over the controlling share of the media, the politicians would have found this unacceptable! The question is 'what do they do about it?' They can't prevent someone carrying out legitimate business. They can't nationalise the media—although some politicians would prefer that option. There is a labour government in power that are distinctly right of centre dealing with a media mogul that appears to support them. A tough decision, but they cannot allow him to become too powerful. Not the media.

So what do they do? Well, how about this for a scenario that will please the conspiracy theorist in all of us and also allow us to wag our righteous fingers at the nasty politicians?

Let us face it. Politicians are a dishonest lot. The only reason that they can climb the greasy pole is because they are, themselves, slimy. They connive, they scheme, they make sure others take the fall for their cock-ups, and the best of them are always deniable. To take on a politician, you have to be dirtier than they are, and there are none too many people who can boast that.

We only have to look at the expenses scandal. Who honestly did not think that they were making dodgy expense claims and have been for years? Even I, with my serious lack of political knowledge, was aware about many of them sharing office space in Westminster with their colleagues and therefore sharing the costs. All MPs are entitled to claim for office space, bearing in mind that the majority have constituencies miles outside London. It would be unreasonable to expect to carry out their legitimate political duties within Westminster without somewhere to work.

The problem comes when they then start claiming rent as if they were paying the full whack. This is common practise, I'm told. Strange that nothing has been said about this anomaly. It couldn't possibly be that the whips that are investigating this are doing the same thing. To bring this to light would seriously damage their expenditure. But the police are now involved in the 'scandal', and many politicians are finding themselves contemplating their navels in Ford Open Prison or having a very uncomfortable time waiting for justice to take its course. Of course, the media have been, by and large, of one mind on this issue, and the politicians have been unable to extricate themselves. Imagine if they were of one mind in all subjects.

THE SCENARIO

Politician—and we are talking high up in the pecking order—sidles up to Winnie, tells him that the government are not too happy about his manoeuvrings, and advise him that it would be in his best interests to back out at this early stage. There are no overt threats, no histrionics, just back off and keep what you have now.

Winnie, who is not used to taking 'advice', thinks to himself, *Who does he think he is trying to cut me off before I have got started?* So he not only ignores the advice but ups his game.

Politician, who is not surprised by this, will have already had something in mind. It has to be something that will hurt our friend, Winnie, but he can't get the rest of the media adversely involved. Of course, the rest of the media aren't particularly enamoured with Winnie because they are in danger of being sidelined if he gets too powerful. This can only mean that they are potential allies. Politicians are always trying to get the media on side, so they are well practised at it (if not always all that successful). The media would need to be aware about what the politicians want to do so that they can ensure that they don't get caught in the same net. At the same time, it needs to be made known that it is in the interests of the media in general and that going outside of the political brief could spoil the plan, so they really do need to be on side and in agreement.

It only remains to put into place the plan. In this case, it surrounds phone hacking! Nice and simple. It is illegal, so he can't tell people that he wasn't dishonest. He is in ultimate control of his empire, so the old 'I was not told' or 'I didn't know' wouldn't work. And it *was* happening, so getting proof would be easy enough. The only thing was making sure the rest of the media could duck out of the way. They are involved up to their grubby necks themselves, but they aren't becoming dangerous. They are, however, allies!

So a little snippet gets out to the press that Winnie's newspaper journalists are hacking phones. There's nothing too over the top, just a few politicians and celebs sticking parts of their anatomy where they don't belong. Stir up a minimedia frenzy so that everyone can beat their breasts about it. Get it to a point where there is a definite offence being alleged and ensure that police are involved, preferably at a high level. The anti-terrorist branch would do. They use phone hacking in their business, and they can just about get away with justifying an investigation.

Make sure that there is a senior police officer involved. This should be easy enough. Anyone DAC or above are looking at the top job and most will do as they are told if that carrot was waved in front of their noses. The great thing about all ambitious people is that one will always get productivity out of them while having leverage, especially if you hold the key to their ambitions.

Allow the investigation to progress to a point and then pull the plug. Essentially, tell the police that there is too much going on—what with the 7/7 bombing and the current critical threat level. Investigating a few dodgy phone hacks about celebrity infidelity is not good use of police resources, so get the DAC to tell everyone that they are no longer investigating for whatever reason. Make sure that it is the decision of the police to end the investigation. Remain deniable, just in case. Throwing the odd police officer to the wolves when things go tits-up is never a bad thing and often good for political kudos. Once this has been done, politician sidles up to Winnie and tells him that it would *really* be in his best interest to back off. This was a little demonstration into what can be if he was not going to be reasonable.

The politician is in a position of strength now. He has half an investigation that was conducted by police. He has a police decision to stop the investigation, and he knows that he has something on his adversary.

Winnie thinks about this for a while. He has a little pow-wow with his top people. He is not trying to mitigate any potential fall out. He is more aggressive than that. He will be planning his next move. In the meantime, there is a change of government—one that has a weakened mandate. This should make it easier for him to throw his weight around. He is thinking that the politicians have picked on the wrong bloke. He is not used to being told, so he decides to call their bluff. Where is the risk? Would the politicians really do this? If they did, in Winnie's mind, they would have to bring the entire media industry to its knees. They are all at it after all. And who else would follow? How many politicians would come crashing down? No, it's a bluff. And how do you answer a bluff? There is only one way: go for the jugular! Be aggressive, and make a decisive move! So he decides to make a move on getting control of 60 per cent of the TV news coverage. Along with his newspaper empire, this would make him unstoppable.

Winnie is bull-headed. He has become successful by confronting head-on. He is too arrogant to believe that anyone would slip under his radar nor does he ever consider that no one will have his back watched—bread and butter to your top politician.

Politician sees this happening and is genuinely narked off that it has come to this. He is of a different political hue to the one who started the ball rolling, but when it comes to media power, there is no compromise. Everything has been set-up nicely. Winnie wants to play hardball, so let's shake the bag and see what falls out. What we do not want is a huge splash of revelations all at once. That would not do the trick.

A big, strong storm that will blow out in a couple of days is not what we have in mind here, oh no! A little story here; another revelation there; build momentum and make each one a little worse, build to a crescendo; ensure that the public is going to be horrified; make sure that the victims of the phone hacking (because we are still running with this) are going to pull at the public heartstrings; make sure the rest of the media are behind you. What's better than to have the media pumping out revelations about the nastiness of the media? Newspapers hacking victims of murder and terrorist atrocities—that will do nicely! Young, innocent murder victims that have been subject to media attention in the recent past—that would be even better.

Politician thinks, 'Let's have a public enquiry.' He can ask prominent members of Winnie's staff to explain how they got their information. No one would have expected anyone to admit to bribing police for info. How outrageous! How well played right into his hands! This means that he has more offences. He also has another set of fall guys.

Oh, and he *will* have to get the police involved again. How is he going to manage that after they have already investigated and found nothing? The public don't know that it is a political decision to stop the investigation so it can remain a police decision. All he now has to do is cast aspersions about the making of that decision, and come across as being outraged that the investigation was stopped without getting to the bottom of it. Make sure that everyone knows that this is an example of police incompetence. They can take the fall for it. He can be self-righteous and ask searching questions about why they did such a botched job of the first investigation. This would force their hand into reopening the investigation. In addition, as the previous investigation was dropped so publicly, the opening of this one can be equally as public, all the while everyone is asking why the police were taking bribes from the media—Winnie's media in particular! Their credibility is shot. They are in a hole, and they have forgotten to stop digging. The rest of the media are doing a fine job in both dragging up more revelations on Winnie and trashing the police. Serves them right for investigating our perfectly reasonable expense claims.

So what do we have now? A long, established newspaper that dealt with titillation and gossip has gone, closed down by the boss as having no place in today's society. A couple of high-flying executives have the tin-tack, but they will get a nice little golden handshake and will have no trouble in seeking further employment if they ever need to work again.

A couple of police officers have bitten the bullet (metaphorically, of course). They are ten a penny, especially the commissioned ranks. Anyone of DAC or above will be looking for the top position and will bend over and take whatever they are told to take if they want that top position.

Then there is the rest of the media. So far, they have managed to slip away from the limelight. We all know that they were as bad as anyone else, but we need a healthy media who take different sides. They then effectively cancel themselves out, allowing politicians to get on with their shenanigans.

As for Winnie and his corporation, he seems to be backing off now. The bid to take over the TV side of the media is on hold, if not dead in the water. He won't like it. He may even have more tricks up his sleeve. His newspaper had a following, and now there is a gap in the market that will be filled very quickly probably by Winnie. We wait with breath abated to see what the next move will be. Will it be Winnie's? Will he knock his king over and concede? Unlikely. Will it be decisive? Maybe, but I don't think so. Perhaps sacrifice a few more pawns in order to manoeuvre himself back into a position of strength (he wouldn't want to sacrifice any more major players, no one would want to work for him if that happened).

I have no doubt that it will be something, and I think it will creep up on us, and I would say that the other media companies better be on their mettle. He has no allegiances, he has been taken apart, and his media rivals have been complicit. He will want them to have their come-uppance. He was, after all, not doing anything that they weren't doing, so why should they walk away with a smug look on their face?

Watch this space.

Printed in Great Britain
by Amazon